♀ Simultaneous Orgasm ♂

For those of you who think "taking turns" is a fact of life, simultaneous orgasm can be liberating. Experiencing orgasm simultaneously defuses the tensions that build up around the question, "Who's going to come first this time?" It brings you into the moment—brings you and your lover into each other—and it focuses you on the essence of your relationship and connection. It releases your power to forge intimate, enduring bonds. Ultimately, it is the great equalizer in bed.

With this book you and your partner will embark on a journey of sexual exploration. Learning to tune into each other sexually is a delicious process. Once you open the pleasure channels in your own body and become practiced at sustaining heightened arousal, then you will be able to come together anytime you want.

The sensual awareness method you will learn in this book will teach you how to ride the waves of arousal higher and higher. You will learn how to prolong pleasure, how to climb to new heights, and how to surrender fully to orgasm. Best of all the sexual skills you build in the process of teaching your bodies to experience simultaneous orgasm will bring you intense levels of pleasure and will develop greater intimacy between you and your partner.

Simultaneous Orgasm

& Other Joys of Sexual Intimacy

Michael Riskin, Ph.D.
&
Anita Banker-Riskin, M.A.

with Deborah Grandinetti

Copyright ©1997 by Michael Riskin, Ph.D., and Anita Banker-Riskin, M.A.

All rights reserved. No part of this publication may be reproduced or transmitted in any form or by any means, electronic or mechanical, including photocopying and recording, or introduced into any information storage and retrieval system without the written permission of the copyright owner and the publisher of this book. Brief quotations may be used in reviews prepared for inclusion in a magazine, newspaper, or for broadcast. For further information, please contact:

Hunter House Inc., Publishers
P.O. Box 2914
Alameda CA 94501-0914

Library of Congress Cataloging-in-Publication Data
Riskin, Michael.
Simultaneous orgasm : and other joys of sexual intimacy /
Michael Riskin, Anita Banker-Riskin. – 1st ed.
p. cm.
Includes bibliographical references and index.
ISBN 0-89793-222-6 (cloth). – ISBN 0-89793-221-8 (paper)
1. Orgasm. 2. Sex. I. Banker-Riskin, Anita. II. Title.
HQ31.R626 1997
613.9'6—dc21   97-19824
CIP

Ordering

Hunter House books are available at bulk discounts for textbook course adoptions; to qualifying community, healthcare, and government organizations; and for special promotions and fundraising. For details please contact:

Special Sales Department
Hunter House Inc., PO Box 2914, Alameda CA 94501-0914
Tel. (510) 865-5282 Fax (510) 865-4295
e-mail: marketing@hunterhouse.com
Individuals can order our books from most bookstores or by calling toll-free:
1-800-266-5592

Project editor: Dana Weissman   Editorial assistant: Belinda Breyer
Production coordinator: Wendy Low
Copy editor: Kathy Hashimoto   Proofreader: Virginia Simpson-Magruder
Cover design: Madeleine Budnick   Book design: Paul J. Frindt
Sales & marketing: Corrine M. Sahli   Marketing associate: Susan Markey
Customer support: Christina Arciniega, Edgar M. Estavilla, Jr.
Business Management: Mike Nealy
Order fulfillment: A & A Quality Shipping Services
Publisher: Kiran S. Rana

Printed and bound by Data Reproductions, Auburn Hills, MI
Manufactured in the United States of America

9 8 7 6 5 4 3 2 1   First Edition

Contents

Introduction	The Orgasm That Nature Favors	1
Part One	**Knowing You Can**	
Chapter 1	The Accidental Simultaneous Orgasm Is No Accident	9
Chapter 2	Kinsey's Reversal: The Real Reason Why	25
Chapter 3	It's Stupendous . . . Cosmic . . . and Within Your Grasp	39
Part Two	**Learning How**	
Chapter 4	Before Play: Laying the Groundwork for Great Sex	59
Chapter 5	Pleasure-Enhancing Control: A Program for Men	77
Chapter 6	Pleasure-Enhancing Release: A Program for Women	113
Chapter 7	Maximizing Your Pleasure: Mastering the Multiple Orgasm	145
Part Three	**Enhancing the Bond**	
Chapter 8	And Now, the Moment You've All Been Waiting For	165
Chapter 9	Don't Make Lust Last, Make It First!	185
	Bibliography	207
	Recommended Reading	209
	Appendix	214
	Index	217

List of Exercises

Chapter 3	Exploring Your Adolescent Sexuality: It's Better the Second Time Around!	43
	Exploring Your Adolescent Sexuality as a Couple: Part One	48
	Exploring Your Adolescent Sexuality as a Couple: Part Two	51
	The Back Caress	54
Chapter 5	The Basic Genital Caress	82
	Tuning in to Your Arousal	85
	The Arousal Awareness "Squeeze"	86
	Learning to Peak	87
	Basic Arousal Awareness à Deux	89
	Start and Stop: Peaking with a Partner	90
	Peaking with the PC Muscle by Yourself	92
	Peaking with the PC Muscle Your Way	93
	Climbing Higher and Higher with Your PC "Brake"	94
	Peaking with a Partner: Part Two	95
	Partner Peaking: An Advanced Variation	96
	Plateauing by Yourself: Breathing	97
	Plateauing by Yourself: PC Squeeze	98
	Plateauing by Yourself: Switching Strokes	99
	Plateauing by Yourself: Changing Your Focus	99
	Creating Plateaus with Your Partner	102
	Side-to-Side Loving	104
	Using the PC Muscle for Control	105
	The Trident Position	107
	Plateauing with Intercourse	108
Chapter 6	Reconnecting with Sexuality, Reawakening Desire: A Guided Imagery Exercise	118
	Cognitive Steps to Greater Sexual Freedom	121
	Vaginal Orgasms	127
	Peaking and Plateauing	132
	Fake It till You Make It	136

	Towel over His Face	137
	Distract the Distraction	138
	The High Rider	139
Chapter 7	Sensate Focus in Service of the Multiple Orgasm	149
	Practicing with Your Partner	152
	Multiple Orgasms with Intercourse	153
	Ask Your Partner for More Support	153
	Solo Ejaculation Awareness	157
	Ejaculation Awareness with Your Partner	158
	Solo Multiple Orgasm	159
	Multiple Orgasm with Your Partner	160
Chapter 8	The Dress Rehearsal	169
	Making the Multiple Simultaneous Orgasm	181
Chapter 9	Ask for What You Want: Version 1	188
	Ask for What You Want: Version 2	190
	Tom Jones Dinner	191
	Your Inner Guide	193
	Blind Walk	193
	Bondage and Domination	194
	The Penile-Vaginal Morse Code Tap	195
	Switching Focus with Yourself	196
	Switching Focus with Your Partner	196
	Switching Focus with Your Partner during Mutual Oral Sex	197
	Nonverbal Communication Using Your Hands	198
	Mutual Masturbation: Pleasing Yourself— Together	200
	Individual Fantasy Exercise	202
	Sharing a Fantasy with Your Partner	202
	Erotic Activities and Fantasies	203
	Stream of Consciousness: The Ultimate Trust and Intimacy Builder	204

Acknowledgments
Who We Are and Why We Presume to Enter Your Bedroom

The book you are now holding represents the collaboration of several individuals. So, if at times you hear distinct voices arising from the text, don't fear; you are not crazy. It is simply because we have respected each other's unique style and wisdom while making this book as useful to you as possible. In other words, we have honored and celebrated the bonding of our differences, just as we ask you to do in the context of your own relationships. Of course, collaborating on a book is not exactly the same as simultaneous orgasm, but it sure felt good when we finished.

Here is the team: The clients of the Riskin-Banker Psychotherapy Center, who were the inspiration for everything in this book.

Michael Riskin, Ph.D., MFCC, board certified sex therapist, and the founding partner of the Riskin-Banker Psychotherapy Center. His ideas, perseverance, and enthusiasm for this project gave it its generative force. His specialty and ongoing interest is helping men unearth and live out their gift of masculinity.

> Writing this acknowledgment section made me aware of something very important. It is the re-realization that Anita and I are still crazy in heat and love for one another after all these years. It's like we really put our money where our mouth is—you know, the old "practice what you preach" concept.
>
> Just two days ago, we returned from a trip to Las Vegas where we renewed our wedding vows at the Graceland Chapel—complete with Elvis, me in my hand-painted "Rock and Roll Forever" jacket and she in one of her very hot, black, clingy dresses that gets me insane with desire. There we were, all teary and barely able to speak the vows. How appropriate, in this year of the publication of our book about the nurturing of relationships and sexuality.

I am a very lucky person because my life has turned out to be far better than I ever thought possible. This required lots of risk-taking—especially with Anita—but it was worth it. Go ahead and take a chance or two yourself.

Anita Banker-Riskin, M.A., MFCC, and board certified sex therapist, is the executive director of the Riskin-Banker Psychotherapy Center. Conceptually and practically, this book simply would not exist without her extraordinary efforts. Anita never faltered in her professional dedication and loving encouragement of everyone in this project. She has helped many women open more ardently to their sexual potential.

Having no prior experience and a great deal of self-doubt, I found writing my part in this book difficult and scary. When bogged down, I followed my own advice and practiced positive self-talk, relaxing, and facing the fear.

I try to live by the principles of this book on a daily basis. The continuing focus of my life is to align the earthy, animal part of me with the intellectual side, and life keeps getting better.

At times, Michael can be very annoyingly male when I'm not in the mood, and annoyingly unmale when I am in the mood. But more often, his maleness and my femaleness come together. Most importantly (especially in times of real crisis), I know he loves me a lot.

Anita and Michael are husband and wife, parents, business partners, and co-authors who continually celebrate the bonding of their differences at many levels. Personally, they can tackle this subject because they enjoy simultaneous orgasms on a regular basis. Professionally, they have worked together for many years as partners and co-therapists treating couples in search of a better life.

Deborah Grandinetti, with a university degree in journalism (and an honorary degree in the human spirit, granted by the universe), is our

Acknowledgments

friend and superstar editor. Designated as "with" on the cover, she was truly with us the entire way. She took mountains of our written and recorded material and sculpted it into a professional work, guiding us from the proposal stage to the completed manuscript. Deborah has collaborated on twenty books, two of which have been bestsellers.

> When Michael and Anita asked me to help write this book for Hunter House, I had a full-time writing job. The prospect of spending evenings and weekends alone at the computer writing about sex didn't especially stir me. But when they said they would not go ahead without me, how could I say no? Two people who are still hot for each other after eighteen years of marriage really have something worthwhile to say, especially in an age when divorce statistics are so high.

Alicia Snelen, M.A., our dear and wonderful friend and colleague has worked as a therapy aide to the center for thirteen years. She performs the vital role of a non-judgmental educator, allowing unpartnered clients to maintain their dignity and improve their self-image while exploring their sexuality. Along with grand insights and reflections about men and women, she provided the detailed instructions for several exercises. Who could be better qualified than Alicia, having personally carried out some of them over a thousand times?

> Thanks to my parents, who raised me with unfailing encouragement, trust, love, and respect, I grew up believing I could be and do anything I wanted.
> Working with Michael and Anita for thirteen years afforded me the privilege of being part of a unique therapeutic team. I thank my clients for placing their trust in me and allowing me to participate in their journeys. Their determination and accomplishments are testimony to the resilience of the human spirit.

Claudia Miles, M.A., is Deborah's assistant. She is building her own psychotherapy practice in Northern California. The stylist of many "short takes," her presence is felt in little jewels sprinkled throughout the book.

Phillip Plotkin, M.A., is Anita's intern and office do-it-all. He is the ever-calming influence who kept on ministering practicality while the rest of us had fits.

It is customary for the author to make mention of his or her publishing support. In our case it is joyful.

To *Kiran Rana:* because you told us things you weren't sure we wanted to hear.

To *Dana Weissman:* because you listened to things we weren't sure you wanted to hear.

To *Lisa Lee:* because you took the time to know the book before you edited the book.

To *Corrine Sahli:* because you focused on nothing but success.

Special mention goes to Mom Jeanette—mother and grandma supreme—and to Cousin Minna—artist, musicologist, and lecturer—just because we love them.

And finally, love, hugs, and thanks to our children, Laura and Jeff, who good-naturedly tolerated us while we tried to figure out how to be effective parents (a skill far more difficult to master than simultaneous orgasms).

This book has been created with the goal of helping you make your love life better, no matter what your starting point, by sharing what we have learned. We hope your experience with *Simultaneous Orgasm* is a good one; we know it has been good for us. We eagerly encourage your ideas and comments!

Foreword

I am very pleased to have been asked to write the foreword to *Simultaneous Orgasm and Other Joys of Sexual Intimacy* by Michael Riskin and Anita Banker-Riskin. My words come from a place of unreserved professional regard for their work, and personal respect for their integrity.

Michael and Anita trained me to work as a surrogate partner in 1980, and we have had a successful professional affiliation for more than fifteen years. Although I consider them to be the "Masters and Johnson of the West Coast," they have achieved conceptual and practical advances far beyond those of other sex therapy practitioners.

For more than twenty years, Michael and Anita have inventively and effectively treated a vast array of clinical problems for many single people and couples. But what makes them even more special is the manner in which they have helped otherwise "normal" clients achieve yet greater degrees of relationship joy and fulfillment. In a field where professional burnout is common, Michael and Anita retain a sense of joy and wonder about sexuality that they convey to the reader.

There are many "how-to" sex books available. What makes this book particularly important is that, as effective as Michael and Anita's techniques may be, its usefulness is not only in fixing problems. Among the strongest and most unique implications is the focus on gender imperatives—how men and women can come to a relationship from equal positions of personal strength, while mutually respecting and honoring the differences that distinguish them as men and women.

Anyone who is part of a couple or who desires to be will gain something valuable from *Simultaneous Orgasm*. Of all the books Michael and Anita could have written, I am glad they wrote this one; it is an important and necessary addition to the existing literature in this dynamic field.

Barbara Keesling, Ph.D.
Newport Beach, 1997

This book is dedicated to our sister, Gail,
and pussycat, Nowheres.

Important Note

This book is directed, for the most part, at the reader whose preference is heterosexual. Why? Simply because that is where the majority of our knowledge base, gathered over twenty years of research and clinical practice, lies. You will read about the celebration and bonding of *gender-based differences*, including those sexual, emotional, and practical factors inherent to a heterosexual relationship. When we refer to the *gender imperative*, we speak of innate demands that need to be recognized and satisfied for men and women to enhance not only their own individual lives, but the quality of their heterosexual relationships as well. However, this is not to say that *Simultaneous Orgasm* is for heterosexual couples exclusively. Some of the sexual potential exercises, relationship and intimacy building suggestions, and the descriptions of male and female physiology are *orientation neutral*. Those will be applicable and useful to gay and lesbian couples as well.

Whatever your preference, we hope you will benefit greatly from what we have to offer.

Introduction
The Orgasm That Nature Favors

Life sometimes brings wonderful and unexpected pleasures. One such pleasure came in the form of "... If Sex Is Good For Her," an article we found in the *Los Angeles Times* around Valentine's Day last year.[1] This little treasure proved something controversial that we had suspected for a long time: There is a biological purpose for female orgasm and simultaneous orgasm, after all!

With men, the biological purpose is obvious: Without the muscular contractions of orgasm and the pleasurable gush of ejaculation, sperm would have a much harder time navigating the distance to the ovum, and conception might never happen. On the other hand, if women don't need to reach orgasm to conceive, why would nature instill such a powerful orgasmic reflex in women, making it easy, in fact, for them to enjoy multiple orgasms in rapid succession? What evolutionary purpose is being served?

In the absence of solid evidence, many theories flourished. Some therapists went so far as to suggest that the female orgasm served evolution by making sex more pleasurable for men, giving them all the more reason to seek it out. (We believe the pleasure *women* experience makes sex more available to men!)

But now scientists have found evidence that female orgasm facilitates fertilization. Studies show that "the female orgasm . . . when timed properly in relation to a man's ejaculation . . . pulls in and retains greater number of sperm."[2] Another researcher found that women who climax up to a minute before or just shortly after their partners retain markedly more sperm than they do following nonorgasmic sex.

In an interesting aside, the scientists concluded that "a woman can influence her reproductive fate by deciding whether to turbocharge the sperm cells of this particular partner." In other words, the muscular contractions of orgasm greatly assist the sperm in propelling themselves up toward the ovum.

When we read that, well . . . the earth moved! What better evidence could we give you that simultaneous orgasm is not only natural but *favored* by nature? For us, this research closed the last open link between simultaneous orgasm and what we call gender imperatives—the biological urges that drive us as sexual beings: the urges to reproduce, give birth, and sustain new life.

As sex therapists and as husband and wife, we know that intercourse nurtures deep emotional bonds between lovers. Simultaneous orgasm, in particular, has a profound, lasting effect on relationships and individuals. Nature knew exactly what it was doing when it designed simultaneous orgasm to nurture emotional bonding and increase the likelihood of conception. The profound union of a man and a woman is a truly awesome way for a child to come into the world, and what better way to ensure the commitment between parents?

Every person can have an orgasm, and every couple can experience it together. This stance runs counter to the position most sex therapists take, and is discussed in depth in Chapter 2.

It is important you know, at the outset, that we do *not* advocate "efforting" in bed. Sexual union should be a place for unbridled expression, joy, and release—not another arena in which you perform. There are many better ways to tie yourself up in knots . . . if you're into that sort of thing!

This is an important point for any of you who fear this book will encourage a performance orientation toward sex or that our approach will destroy any spontaneity you have left in your life. The working world can be a maze of routines, so you have every reason to hold the spontaneous nature of sex sacred. This is why we emphasize: *The art of simultaneous orgasms won't put any more pressure on either of you.* In fact, it is likely to relieve pressure, being in sync with the way nature made us. A simultaneous orgasm is one of the more wonderful ways to celebrate the bonding of masculine and feminine natures.

For those of you who think "taking turns" is a fact of life, simultaneous orgasm can be liberating. Simultaneous climax defuses the tensions that build up around the question, "Who's going to come first this time?" It also eliminates the opportunity and the need to act out sexual dissatisfaction with relationship-sabotaging behaviors. Simultaneous orgasm brings you into the moment, it brings both of you into each other, and it focuses you on the essence of your relationship and connection. It releases your power to forge intimate, enduring bonds. Ultimately, it is the great equalizer in bed, as you will learn in Chapter 1.

We will ask you to try the erotic exercises in this book, but not to pass judgement on yourself or your partner. This book is all about putting you in touch with what your body already knows. Once your body knows how, simultaneous orgasm will happen quite effortlessly. Lovers who experience simultaneous orgasm by accident often don't know how their bodies know, but somehow they do. And the more they experience them, the easier it is to have them.

Here are some key things you should know or expect as you approach this book:

You are embarking on a journey of sexual exploration. Simultaneous orgasms might not happen right away, especially if you and your partner are not sexually attuned to each other. Learning to tune into each other is a delicious process, and once you open the pleasure channels in your own body and become practiced at sustaining heightened arousal, then you will be able to come together easily.

The sensual awareness method you will learn in this book will teach you how to ride the waves of arousal higher and higher, without interrupting your sexual activity. This means you can remain physically connected and experience even deeper pleasures each time you enter a new arousal cycle. You will learn how to prolong pleasure, how to climb to new heights, and how to surrender fully to orgasm. The sexual skills you build in the process of teaching your body simultaneous orgasms will give you more pleasure and greater mastery.

"Choice" is the key word when it comes to sexual pleasure. The sexual techniques in Part Two of this book are all about choice and variety.

These techniques help you become so familiar with your body and your natural sexual style that you can effortlessly sustain the degree of intensity you most desire, for as long as you like. So, if you like to plunge into orgasm with your lover, melting into waves of pleasure as one, you will be able to. If you want to savor the peaks of pleasure without having an orgasm, you can. And, if you'd like to try having one orgasm after another in a rapid-fire sequence of sexual fireworks, you will be able to do that, too. The variety you can bring to your lovemaking will be limited only by your imagination and desire.

There is another powerful and unique aspect of simultaneous orgasm that we want to share with you: *Simultaneous orgasm can be spiritually invigorating and can move you toward a sense of wholeness.*

In a very real and beautiful sense, simultaneous orgasm can bring about that special union that prophets referred to when they wrote of how two shall be as one flesh. The act of intercourse accomplishes this in a literal, physical fashion, but simultaneous orgasm takes you beyond your physical selves to emotional ecstasy. For some couples, it is the gateway into a transcendent, resplendent dimension of human experience.

The mutual vulnerability you reach at the point of climax, when you melt into tensionless bliss together, is a uniquely charged moment. Opening fully to each other's energies helps one become a more integral part of the other. After sharing simultaneous orgasms for a while, you may notice yourself understanding your partner better or taking on his or her strengths. It may be as if you are learning from your lover's body by osmosis, through immersion in the pleasure state that you both lovingly create together.

Wherever simultaneous orgasm takes you and your lover, both of you are sure to be richly rewarded. The process of erotic exploration will be as pleasurable and meaningful as the outcome. So relax, take it slow, luxuriate in the learning as it unfolds, and above all, have fun!

How to Read This Book

Depending on what you want from this book, consider reading the two parts in a way that best addresses your relationship to sexuality. We have organized this book to speak to the needs of your mind, your body, and your emotions.

Part One, "Knowing You Can," will give you information on the cultural background and psychology of coming together—in order to satisfy your mind. As you read these three chapters, try to be honestly open to the possibility of simultaneous orgasm. Once your intellect is convinced that simultaneous orgasm is possible and desirable, it will be easier for your body to experience it.

Part One will also explain the skills of maintaining a committed union and will offer techniques for dealing with the inevitable tensions that arise in intimate relationships. If you never address these tensions, then even the hottest sexual dynamic will fizzle. Women in particular find that lingering hurt, anger, or resentment dampens all sexual desire.[3]

Part Two, "Learning How," describes a series of exercises that will give you and your partner the sensual and physical skills that enable simultaneous orgasm and orgasmic choice. Chapter 5 on ejaculation control is written by Michael, for men; Chapter 6, on female orgasm, is written by Anita, for women. Both chapters go step-by-step through a series of exercises: some are for you and your lover to do separately, and some are for you both to do together. Because men and women are very different when it comes to sex and sexuality, the chapters are very different in their focus and tone. (But don't forget, in difference there is delight!)

We suggest you approach Part Two by reading Chapter 4 together with your partner. Then make a commitment to read through your partner's chapter at least once. This will help you better understand your partner's sexuality. When it's time to read through your own chapter, set up a schedule for doing the exercises that allows time in your regular routine to experiment with the solo exercises. Consult with your partner to set aside time for the exercises you do together. Keep in mind that the exercises are sexual explorations—treat them as an opportunity for learning and pleasure, not as a chore or obligation.

Part Three, "Enhancing the Bond," will help you understand the dynamics that keep your sex life alive. At this point, you may acknowledge that there are times when the profound experience of great sex can help you realize how petty disagreements or begrudgings can be. The trick is to recognize what is trivial and what needs to be confronted in open, honest, and safe communication.

The two chapters in Part Three will help you gain the skills to do this. They provide you with practical tools to emotionally embrace each other and "come together" at every level—physically, mentally, emotionally, and spiritually. Remember, foreplay can be a twenty-four-hour pastime. And it ought to be, for both your lives to come together and to experience the pleasures of love.

What If Your Partner Isn't Interested?

If you would like to try simultaneous orgasms but your partner isn't interested, try leaving this book around for him or her to read. Then after a time, bring up the subject using an "I" statement, such as "Honey, our sex life is very important to me and I would really like to experience simultaneous orgasm. Will you consider trying this with me?"

"I" statements are a great way to broach difficult topics because they don't invite defensive reactions. "You" statements, such as "You never do things for me. Why won't you work with me so that we can have a simultaneous orgasm at least once?" can make anyone dig in their heels and get defensive, if not angry.

If, after discussing it, your partner remains uninterested in achieving simultaneous orgasm, you can still benefit from following these sexual explorations by yourself. By working through this book, you will come to a greater understanding of your sexual desire and sexual potential. You will become attuned to your own pleasure centers and pleasure patterns. And you will better understand the sexual dynamic you and your partner share. So don't be surprised if, after you've done all this, your partner changes his or her mind!

Notes:

1. Kathleen Kelleher, "Odds of Conception May Be Better If Sex Is Good For Her," *Los Angeles Times*, 19 Feb. 1996, sec. E.
2. See note 1 above.
3. The emotional/sexual relationship is a natural reaction, in part the result of women's biochemical makeup. Women have much higher estrogen levels, and estrogen predisposes emotionality. (Men do have small amounts of estrogen.) The higher the estrogen levels, typically, the more emotional the individual. Conversely, the testosterone levels in men predispose them to more emotional detachment.

Part One
Knowing You Can

Chapter 1
The Accidental Simultaneous Orgasm Is No Accident

For love . . . has two faces; one white, the other black; two bodies; one smooth, the other hairy. It has two hands, two feet, two tails, two, indeed, of every member and each one is the exact opposite of the other. Yet, so strictly are they joined together that you cannot separate them.

—Virginia Woolf, *Orlando*

A man and a woman in a garden paradise. According to one of the most enduring parables in history, this is how it all began. The man had power over every beast and bird, but he was still lonely. The woman came into her own when the man was asleep, and they made love. And though they were both naked, they were not ashamed.

If ever there was an archetype with the force of truth, the Garden of Eden is it. It speaks to an innocent age when our relationship to the world was instinctual and sensory. Eden was simple and transplendent. There were no fax machines. No dirty diapers. No hockey games. No smelly socks on the floor. No dripping pantyhose in the bathroom. No toilet seat lids to fight over. No ERA and no Men's Movement.

Our day-to-day lives may seem a far cry from the splendor of Eden, and yet, within the sphere of each truly intimate relationship, the promise of paradise beckons. It is as a grace you can evoke in your togetherness. Sure, there are times when this grace is hidden and elusive, but it never really goes away. Paradise does exist, and it patiently awaits your return.

To get there, together, you must be willing to give it your all. Not just your bodies, but your thoughts and feelings too, the subtle parts of you. You must be willing to throw it all onto the fire of connubial bliss, to suffer the exquisite energy that shoots like sparks along the periphery of your body as the fire inside blazes brighter and hotter. And if you're really courageous, you will let your fires burn as one, encircling you both.

This means reawakening the instinctual self—the sensualist, the reverent one, the adventurer. It means emboldening yourself to embrace the fullness of Eros, opening yourself to the redemptive experience of oneness and knowing that you are not alone, unworthy, or unwanted. What a glorious relief that is. The world around you begins to change. You literally "walk in beauty," as the Native American expression describes it, radiating vitality and peace to everyone you meet.

Are you skeptical? We've seen this power change lives. Everyone has the power to bring about this paradisal love, couple by couple, coitus by coitus. Peace begins at home, it is said, and for committed partners profound sexual love can renew the presence of the sacred in the midst of daily routine. Just think: we can bring peace into the world, two by two, in our conjugal beds—or downstairs, or in the shower, or in the back of that '57 Chevy—when the urge strikes. Each couple can find the way to paradise. Just let the dove of your desire lead the way, and the dove of peace will follow.

Pleasure and Peace between Equals

How can we make the outrageous claim that great sex between committed partners contributes to world peace? Let's look at history. In her pioneering scholarly work, *The Chalice and the Blade*, Riane Eisler did just that and came to some very exciting conclusions. In ancient Crete, where "peace endured for 1,500 years both at home and abroad in an age of incessant warfare," men and women reveled in their sexual differences. As Eisler writes:

> . . . the bare-breasted style of dress for women and the skimpy clothes emphasizing the genitals for men demonstrate a frank

appreciation of the sexual differences and the pleasure made possible by these differences. From what we know now through modern humanistic psychology, this 'pleasure bond' would have strengthened a sense of mutuality between men and women as individuals.[1]

At a time when other, barbaric nation-states were exploring the dynamics of power through domination, the people of ancient Crete "seem to have reduced and diverted their aggressiveness through a free and well-balanced sex-life," according to cultural historian Jacquetta Hawkes.[2] Hawkes, Eisler, and other scholars believe this understanding of sexual differences contributed greatly to the "generally peaceful and harmonious spirit predominant in Cretan life."[3]

What was true for people in ancient Crete is true today. Our many years of research and sex counseling have led us to believe that the only way for men and women to truly live together in harmony is through a frank acknowledgment and appreciation of gender-based differences. While Eisler, Hawkes, and others came to this conclusion through historical research, we arrived at it after counseling thousands of couples with marital or relationship difficulties and after working through our own relationship as a couple. The only way we can create lasting peace within our relationships—the kind that ripples out to the larger world—is to come to a mature acceptance of our fundamental differences. This means recognizing that our differences are in function, not value, as the late Italian psychiatrist Robert Assiagoli, M.D., so eloquently put it.

The passion and the peace of Crete is a choice that every couple will struggle with in their relationship as they balance their power issues, relationship patterns, and baggage from the past. As a culture we must also come together to choose. Are we ready to end the war between the sexes? Certainly, many of us think it has gone on long enough. Can we free sex from the taint of gender betrayal?

When you look at all the evidence, it is clear that neither sex has come out of the gender war unharmed. The motivations and consequences of this war are passed on from generation to generation. As sex, marriage, and family therapists, we have seen a lot of unnecessary suffering. We think it's time for a truce. Yet, as Woodrow Wilson said, only a peace between equals can last. Fortunately, this, too, is beginning to occur in our intimate relationships. The model of marriage as a hierarchical relationship is falling away, just as hierarchical structures are crumbling in the business world. Amidst the chaos, something new is being born.

What is coming into being, through each couple who embraces the change, is a true partnership between equals—one in which couples don't deny their differences but share and delight in them. For some couples this is relatively easy, but for others it is agonizing—and with good reason. How do we know that which we have not learned? Where would men and women have learned how to be equals? After centuries of matriarchal society and centuries more of patriarchal rule, our society has ingrained a "topdog-underdog" dynamic. Our challenge now is to collectively dismantle the old and rearrange the pieces into a new kind of balance between men and women.

Power . . . Surrender . . . Passion!

In the first half of the twentieth century, James Thurber created a popular satirical feature called "The War Between Men and Women." It would have been even funnier if it weren't so true. As sex, marriage, and family therapists, we see the war play itself out in our clinic daily. It is clear that the adversarial spirit of our courts has infiltrated modern relationships. Couples act out the roles of prosecutor and defendant, criminal and victim, winner and loser. The differences between them—often the very qualities that made them so hot for each other at the beginning—are the fuel for their fights. Ironically, these differences could bring greater emotional fulfillment and sexual ecstasy to their relationship.

We'd like to propose an alternative to the fighting: bonding. Bonding both creates and originates from an intimate knowing that transcends our faulty learning. It occurs when two autonomous people come together in safety and vulnerability, in power and surrender. Bonding springs from a mutuality based on trust, respect, and commitment.

Bonding does not mean that two people become one or that one's autonomy is lost to the relationship. This is neither healthy nor desirable. For true bonding to occur, each person must have (or develop) a strong sense of self, healthy boundaries, and a passionate commitment to his or her own self-fulfillment. Their autonomy should grow as a result of the relationship, which values and strengthens who they are as individuals. When we experience ourselves as autonomous within a close relationship in which we feel connected, loved, cherished, and respected, we thrive—we are profoundly fulfilled. Despite the "war between the sexes," deep down this is really what most of us want. The good news is that it is within our reach.

One of the reasons why a loving bond seems so hard to create in intimate relationships today is because we are confused about what it means to be a man or a woman. We have lost touch with who we are as masculine and feminine beings. Not coincidentally, cultures that have initiatory rites of passage for men and women and mating rituals do not have this problem. What has happened to our society?

We have forgotten the essential principles of masculinity and femininity, and we fail to honor the differences. Part of our confusion comes from being caught between the old and the new: the biological imperatives we share with every other animal species and our uniquely human consciousness, our transcendent brain, which is still evolving. The pull between our ancient wiring and modern minds distresses us, and our relationships invariably reflect that internal struggle. We want to be powerful (but accepted), vulnerable (but not taken advantage of), independent (but not ignored), nurtured (but not dominated), desired (but not made into sex objects). We don't always know how to strike a balance or what we can and should expect from the other.

So why all of this talk of masculinity, femininity, and gender-based bonding in a book about enjoying better sex? Because grasping these ideas will introduce you to *awesome* sex, complete with the elusive, misunderstood, and coveted simultaneous orgasm.

The purpose of this book is not to go into the subject of gender in detail, but to enhance the quality of your sexual relationships with specialized information and practical techniques. Many scholarly and popular works deal with all imaginable aspects of gender differences. One excellent book is *What Women & Men Really Want*. [Kipnis, A., Ph.D. and Herron, E., M.A. (Novato, CA: Nataraj Publishing, 1995.) pp. 279–290] However, a few gender-based ideas directly affect the quality of sexual relationships.

A simultaneous orgasm represents the reward for being in tune with one's sexual nature. Sexually, the male instinct is to pursue, court, seduce, become erect, penetrate, thrust, and ejaculate. A man seeks a desirable mate who demonstrates selectivity in her choice of partners, who will remain sexually loyal and nurture his children. Physiologically, he needs to "get the job done"; psychologically, he needs to have the confidence to enable it.

The woman who is available to his pursuit, courtship, and seduction recognizes herself as the radiant force that draws her lover to her. She knows she's worthy of being wooed, even after she's been won. She embraces her sexuality and respects it too much to treat it as a commodity to control. She knows how to get her needs met without making him feel inadequate. She is secure in her desirability, unafraid to stand up to him when her own self-respect is at stake.

Deciding to enjoy a simultaneous orgasm with a particular man represents nature's granting her the ultimate power and choice over who will become the father of her children. Physiologically, she also needs to "get the job done." Psychologically, she needs to feel both her own desirability and his intense desire for her, along with his commitment to the relationship. Furthermore, a woman who is in touch with her erotic self controls her own orgasmic response, selecting whom she will allow to pull its trigger.

Why are these needs and instincts so powerful? From a Darwinian perspective, they are part of the programming built into us that keeps the species going. As you know, the instinct to "be fruitful and multiply" is second only to the instinct to survive. Nature gave the male of the species the mandate to spread his seed. The female of the species may best ensure survival by being choosy, and sticking around with her lucky selection to help protect and provide for the offspring. A relationship that satisfies these instinctual needs for both partners is likely to be mutually satisfying, complete with intense bonding and simultaneous orgasm.

As we said earlier, there is much more to be read and talked about on this subject, which often generates much discussion during our lectures and interviews. The ramifications are sweeping as they affect many other aspects of life. By affirming one's masculinity or femininity, simultaneous orgasm can bolster identity and sense of self.

Sharing Power and Respect

A man has a fundamental need to feel powerful within the relationship. That's what validates him as a masculine being. Yet, he can only feel that power when his partner is willing to accept it. Otherwise, sex is masturbation for him at best and rape at worst. A woman has just as strong a need to feel desired and cherished as well as powerful within her relationship. This is what affirms her as a feminine being. But even that is not enough to arouse her. She can only feel satisfied when her partner brings her adequacy-based power. Otherwise, sex becomes genital availability at best and victimization at worst. But when the power is shared, the sparks of the opposites can fly.

We call this psychosexual dynamic the "power-cherish dynamic." It is absolutely archetypal. A beautiful illustration of it appears in the movie *Moonstruck,* when a middle-aged couple makes love. She says to him, "You were like a tiger." He replies, "You were soft like a lamb." The power of vulnerability and desire form the basis of our sexual experience, and our differences in experiencing them are what make sexual relationships so wonderful.

Healthy bonding can only take place when a man and woman both feel empowered and respect each other as equals. In our evolving social structure, men are having the hardest time with this, while women experience the brunt of it. We believe that men ultimately find fulfillment in having power within themselves, not over others. A powerful male is one who feels he can deal effectively with the world around him without trying to make anyone his inferior. This is known as the "power to" mindset. Men who feel good about themselves don't need to dominate women.

But when men don't feel powerful within themselves, they may seek "power over," or a dominance that requires someone else to be a victim, an inferior. This comes out in the behavior of the stereotypical macho man, as well as the man with rescuer/provider tendencies. It may seem at first that this man wants nothing in return for his personal, twenty-four-hour 911 service, but he does have an agenda. In return for rescuing and caretaking, he wants subservience and eternal gratitude. He needs a victim in order to function, and if he can't find one he will try to create one. Still other men swing from one extreme of the power pendulum to the other. They may feel impotent one day and omnipotent the next. When they feel impotent, they act with fear and anxiety. When they feel omnipotent, they act with arrogance, as if they could handle anything.

Women respond positively to male power when it is used to serve them, but not when it is used to intimidate or disempower them. They experience fulfillment with independent partners who can share power and who acknowledge their individual worth. Of course, there are also women who never find the middle ground. Some feel disempowered and seek "power over" by treating their partners as inferior. We have treated couple situations in which she is clearly in control and he is cowering. This is just as unhealthy as the other way around. He will not leave her because his self-esteem and personal power is so low he feels no other woman will have him; she feels alienated and alone because she does not really have a relationship with a partner. By overpowering and smothering, she leaves her receptive feminine nature unfulfilled. Consequently, she and her partner will never share a satisfying sex life.

The Other Sex, Not the Opposite Sex

When men and women perceive each other as opposites, they encourage the war between the sexes. They become adversaries—when one wins, the other loses. The secret to a great relationship is honoring our differences. As we tell our clients, you really only have two choices: cherish or perish. Men and woman are different, and the differences go beyond physiology. Denying male or female differences does not strengthen pair-bonding, nor does speaking of men or women as the opposite sex. The verb form of opposite is "oppose," which means to resist or combat. Why allow the expectation of combativeness to creep into our language and our mindset? Considering each other as the other sex will serve us much better. The exploration of our otherness brings richness, new possibilities, growth, and wholeness to our relationships.

An attitude of openness to male/female differences can cure a lot of relationship ills. How a couple relates to the power-cherish dynamic has profound implications for how successfully they relate to each other, settle differences, and make love. In our therapy sessions we have seen time and again how understanding this dynamic and learning how to put it into practice can help resolve what seem like intractable relationship problems. Take infidelity, for example. Sometimes, when a man looks for sex outside of his primary relationship, it may be because he feels inadequate. When a woman does, it may be because she feels undesirable.

Sexual Epoxy: Building the Bonds That Endure

A wandering eye can also be chalked up to simple evolutionary biology. It was to a man's evolutionary advantage to spread his seed all over town, and it is in a woman's best interest to seek out a partner with the most to invest in offspring. Evolutionary biologists say that nature may have designed us to fall in love but not to stay in love. Of course, it is wholly natural for both men and women to sour on each other at certain times and under certain circumstances, but we think these crises ought to be weathered. A commitment to bonding requires a conscious choice. That choice is easier to sustain, however, when men and women understand each other's primal needs and fulfill them. It is easier still when the sex is great and continues to get better and better!

Through sexual intimacy—honoring and fulfilling our masculine and feminine natures—we can make these biological drives support our long-term, conscious commitment. Our relationship can grow sweeter over the years rather than more estranged. Honoring what is quintessentially male and quintessentially female creates a climate in which simultaneous orgasm is the natural expression of a beautifully balanced relationship.

Coming Together: A Union of Equals

Simultaneous orgasm, not surprisingly, embodies this conscious commitment even as it draws couples closer together. Sexually speaking, the partnership impulse finds its highest expression in mutual climax. It is the great equalizer. It isn't "me first, then you" or "you first, then me" but "us together, sharing an extraordinary experience."

The relationship consequences of simultaneous orgasms are profound. Simultaneous orgasm brings lovers to a place where *both* are vulnerable and open to each other. For a moment, the barriers to bonding dissolve. In lovemaking, lovers dissolve them together.

"To me, it's the ultimate climax between partners," said *Betty*, a sixty-two-year-old widow from Buffalo, one of many people who responded to a survey we conducted on simultaneous orgasm. "I always looked forward to sex, knowing that we would both be fulfilled at the end, together."

"It's spiritual and physical," said *Edward*, a forty-eight-year-old Ohio man. "The sensation of bringing her to climax at the same time I explode is wonderful. I don't have them with my current partner, but I do miss them."

"What's so nice about simultaneous orgasm," said *Alicia*, our very own researcher, "is the emotional connection. You feel like you are caught up in something bigger than both of you—some grand, all-encompassing thing has enveloped you both. It's emotionally unifying."

Discovering Your Soulmate

From what we've discovered during our research, plenty of couples experience simultaneous orgasm spontaneously, without willing it or consciously preparing for it in any way. And although these are considered "accidental," we think they are no accident. It is as if nature is using pleasure to encourage us to stay together as we take on the difficult work of building and sustaining a relationship.

When simultaneous orgasm occurs on the very first date, or with regular frequency in one sexual relationship (but not others), it can mark a relationship as very special. *Alec*, for example, has them consistently with *Joanna*, and though he can't seem to sustain their relationship for long periods of time—they've broken up and reunited many times over the last seven years—he can't get her out of his mind. "I see her face first thing when I wake up in the morning and last thing when I go to bed at night," Alec said, wistfully.

Ellen, a thirty-year-old woman in New Orleans, told us that she has only had simultaneous orgasm with her current boyfriend. "I've never been able to figure out why. My orgasms are more intense with *Antoine* than with anyone I've ever been with. And simultaneous orgasms are the most intense. I've read that people like to take turns so they can enjoy 'their own' orgasm. But that's not true for us. We both love the intensity of coming together!"

Climaxing simultaneously is often a sign of special resonance, a signifier that this relationship is a "keeper." In an age when people hunger for soulmates, a sexual experience this deep can make couples feel they have found theirs. Such was the case for *Allegra*. When the forty-year-old professional writer and speaker experienced simultaneous orgasm the first time she made love with her now-husband, the experience opened her eyes to what they had together. Until that moment, she wasn't convinced he was the man for her.

"I had turned forty and just completed my college degree," she said. "I pictured myself getting involved with an academic or a professional man. I wasn't so sure I wanted to be with a man who worked in the trades, like *Thomas* did. In fact, I resisted him in everything at first, and didn't contact him for three weeks after we had met. But then we started dating. One day, I was housesitting in San Francisco and we had sex. It just happened.

"The power of it all affirmed to me how right the relationship was, on every level," said Allegra. "My soul knew it, my heart knew it—but not my ego. It took the simultaneous orgasm to make me see. What the experience said to me was, 'here is the man for me.' We connect on every level." Allegra and Thomas continue to enjoy simultaneous orgasms. "It's not something we work towards, but it still happens. And when it does, it's spectacular!"

"When you think about it, every time you have sex, you are bringing together the most powerful energy in the universe," said Allegra. "When Thomas and I come together and have a simultaneous orgasm, or just a regular one, we create something beautiful together. The first simultaneous orgasm brought about the birth of our relationship."

We've heard similar stories from couples all across the country who came together the first time they made love and who eventually committed permanently to each other. Imagine what it is like to make love the very first time, to flow together into a mutual, heart-enveloping, soul-stirring climax, instead of working through the usual first-time awkwardness.

"I remember saying to myself at the time, 'We're going to do this again!'" said *Chuck*, a sixty-three-year-old Kansas native who married *Susie*, the first woman with whom he ever experienced a simultaneous orgasm. At the time, he was in another relationship, but he left it and has stayed with Susie ever since. "It really bonds you," said Chuck, while Susie replied with a laugh, "I felt like the earth moved for me! It was really wonderful."

Keith, a thirty-two-year-old New York native, and his partner *Shondra*, a thirty-eight-year-old from Michigan, echo those sentiments. These two shared a simultaneous orgasm on their very first date. Although that was years ago, Keith remembered it well: "It was very exciting. We hadn't experienced one another before, and we went back to my house and made love in the bedroom. It was definitely more special because it was a simultaneous orgasm."

"It was absolutely more special," Shondra affirmed. Although she'd climaxed together with other partners, Shondra said it was never with the same frequency as with Keith. "There has to be electricity or chemistry involved, because we just click in that way."

Even when it's not the first time, the experience of reaching a simultaneous orgasm together can be memorable. "It was magic. I'll never forget it," mused *Wayne*, a thirty-nine-year-old produce manager, as he recalled a relationship that ended fifteen years ago. "I was so in love with her. The one or two times it happened, it really brought us close. It was like, for that space in time, we were completely open to each other. Energetically, spiritually, the whole bit."

Unlocking the Potential

Why is it that some couples ignite immediately and have a simultaneous orgasm the very first time they go to bed together? And why is it that others experience the power of it just once, but never again? Well, the second question is easy. These folks haven't learned conscious control over the process, which you will discover in Part Two of this book. As for the first question, we wish we had a concrete answer. In our experience, coming together has a lot to do with chemistry. The two people may be "soulmates," at least for that phase of their lives. They may work well together because they are gifted at egalitarian relations. Sometimes, they are simply in sync with each other sexually.

What we do concretely know is that real people, from all walks of life, speak about spontaneous simultaneous orgasms from experience. That's important to remember. Once you know that other couples have them, easily and without special training, it stands to reason that they exist within the range of normal human sexual experience. And that means that they are a distinct possibility for you.

Isn't that worth celebrating? It is awesome when you stop to consider how human sexual expression has evolved: from the rear-entry primate quickie to a spiritually powerful, face-to-face, mutually orgasmic, many-houred extravaganza.

So why not allow yourselves the pleasure? Why not be open to a sexual experience that, as one twenty-seven-year-old Indiana man said, is "out of this world"? Just think. In addition to drawing closer to each other, you might help to bring a whole new world into being. Crete—like Eden, the original pleasure garden—is only a memory away.

Notes

1. Riane Eisler, *The Chalice and the Blade: Our History, Our Future* (San Francisco: HarperCollins, 1987), 39.
2. Jacquetta Hawkes, *Dawn of the Gods: Minoan and Mycenaean Origins of Greece* (New York: Random House, 1968), 153.
3. Ruby Rohrilich-Leaven, "Women in Transition: Crete and Sumer," in *Becoming Visible*, ed. Renate Bridenthal and Claudia Koonz (Boston: Houghton Mifflin, 1977), 49, 46.

Chapter 2
Kinsey's Reversal: The Real Reason Why

Nature never deceives us; it is always we who deceive ourselves.

—Jean Jacques Rousseau, *Emile*

If simultaneous orgasm is so wonderful, why haven't you heard much about it before? Why have women's magazines, which never hesitate to use cover teasers like "Six Sexual Secrets to Keep Him Begging for More," kept silent on the subject? Why have men's magazines dismissed it?

The prestigious Kinsey Institute slammed the simultaneous orgasm in 1990, completely reversing a position it had taken for years. In doing so, it took the position most sex therapists have taken since the mid-1960s—that simultaneous orgasms aren't worth the time and attention.

The Kinsey people had it right the first time, but the growing, pervasive relationship problems people were having influenced the sex therapy industry. In 1953, the Institute explained that simultaneous orgasm, for most people, represents the "maximum achievement which is possible in a sexual relationship."[1] But, in 1990, a new Kinsey Institute publication declared: "It's a myth that simultaneous orgasms should occur, that this is an important part of marital happiness, or that it is even desirable as a sexual pattern. Simultaneous orgasms are not common, and in fact, probably not worth striving for."[2] What happened between 1953 and 1990? Had men and women changed all that much in forty years, or did the experts have reason to reassess their thinking?

What happened was political: sex therapists realized the prevalence of sexual problems in America and backed down. The reversal was a tacit admission of failure by the "experts," who recognized that some very basic sexual problems were not being effectively treated. Without adequately addressing those basic problems, simultaneous orgasm was out of the question.

So what is happening in the 1990s? About half of all women in this country can't reach orgasm during intercourse, and, according to the most conservative estimates, about 60 percent of men ejaculate prematurely. Impotence is also common, and many men have performance-related anxiety. These are *entirely treatable* problems, but not every therapist knows the proven treatments or is willing to use them. For example, in one seminar we recently attended, a sex therapist who has authored several technical books and is highly regarded in the professional community expounded on his methods to resolve premature ejaculation. When someone asked him about the "PC squeeze" technique (covered in Chapter 5), lacking any knowledge or experience of the technique, he dismissed it. "Oh that—it doesn't really work," he said. Yet we know of thousands of men who no longer ejaculate prematurely, and they and their partners would certainly disagree with that therapist. Our clients have had tremendous success with it.

Given these problems, the sex therapy community figured that devaluing simultaneous orgasm was the "kind" and easy thing to do. Their rationalization was: why talk about simultaneous orgasm if he can't control the timing of his ejaculation and she can't orgasm during intercourse and we barely have the know-how to change that? Why frustrate people further?

Sadly, this line of thinking leaves the impression that there is no alternative to sequential orgasm, in which lovers climax separately. It prevents most people from knowing about a very possible, very pleasurable alternative. And because many of us tend to believe the experts, their attitudes filter into the wider culture. Even educated people make such misguided comments as "More experienced and sensitive lovers enjoy their partner's climactic transports, which they are unable to do if they orgasm simultaneously." (Would the author of this statement also find shared laughter insensitive, or would he recommend that a couple take turns watching the sunset rather than enjoy its beauty together, so as not to appear insensitive?)

Worthier, still, of critical comment is Thomas Szaz's remark in the *The Second Sin* that simultaneous orgasm is a "a psychiatric-sexual myth useful for fostering feelings of sexual inadequacy and personal inferiority. It is also a rich source of psychiatric 'patients.'" What really leads to such emotional distress (and a thriving psychotherapy practice) is the lack of profound, intimate bonds between partners. Ironically, simultaneous orgasm is a strong means of forging these bonds. The couples we have interviewed and worked with over the years emphasize this again and again. In our own experience, as lovers and as husband and wife, we *know* it to be true.

Michael had concurred with the majority opinion until the mid-1970s when a series of events occurred to change his mind. First, in his clinical practice (now specializing in sex therapy), he began to hear reports from couples describing simultaneous orgasms in their sex lives. Similar events were taking place at that time in his own social life. Meanwhile, he and his colleagues undertook the development of a variety of sex therapy techniques that would eventually facilitate the process outlined in this book. He began to realize what a travesty it has been that most professional literature on sexuality published in the past four decades has condemned simultaneous orgasm for being too difficult, too impractical, and too much work. During this time, how many well-read couples who have never experienced simultaneous orgasm have been mentally conditioned against it?

Another consequence of the party line is that couples who have been fortunate enough to experience simultaneous orgasm once or twice haven't realized that they could experience it at will or that it is possible for them to enjoy *multiple* mutual orgasms. Yes, that's right—men are capable of multiple orgasms, too!

It is time for couples to set their sexual sights higher instead of lower. Having premature ejaculation or inorgasmia (the inability of a woman to reach orgasm with her partner) today doesn't preclude enjoying a simultaneous orgasm next month. The solutions are here—all you need is the commitment. Couples who commit to finding sexual satisfaction discover that miracles can happen.

Kayla came to us because her vaginal muscles were so tight she couldn't tolerate penetration. Kayla and her husband, *Robert*, were newlyweds and very much in love. They consulted different doctors who said they could do little for her. But there was more to this than a medical problem, and we helped Kayla uncover what it was. She learned to relax and enjoy sex, and eventually, she and Robert shared simultaneous orgasms whenever they desired. If it is possible for people like Kayla and Robert to begin without sex and end up with simultaneous orgasms at will, it is possible for just about any couple.

> ## Michael on "What Everyone except the Experts Knows"
>
> Sexual myths and incorrect, out-of-date information are as likely to be fostered by a professional as a nonprofessional. For example, if you ask about the significance of penis size and female satisfaction, virtually all professionals will respond that size is irrelevant because the vagina is a potential space and any penis in a normal developmental range is sufficient to be felt in the vagina. This is quite accurate with two important exceptions: Size is not irrelevant to the woman who enjoys anal penetration. For her, a smaller penis is actually more desirable. Nor is it irrelevant to the woman who has been eroticized to a larger flaccid or erect penis. This acculturation is as real as that of a man who is aroused by breast size.

A New Era of Sexual Understanding

Fortunately, we live in a time when sex therapy is becoming more and more of a practical science. This is relatively new. It wasn't until William Masters and Virginia Johnson published *Human Sexual Response* in 1966, that we had any real science on which to base therapeutic interventions. Theirs was a groundbreaking book: it was the first complete study of the physiology and anatomy of sexuality. (Until you know how something works, it's hard to know how to fix it.) Masters and Johnson went on to develop the first practical, effective treatments to help men and women overcome functional sexual problems. One approach was a method called *sensate focus*, which teaches people to come back to their senses, literally, when anxieties threaten to disrupt their natural sexual functioning. Sensate-focus awareness is a cornerstone for our approach for simultaneous orgasm.

Masters and Johnson made such an impact with their work that sex therapy may be referred to as either "pre–Masters and Johnson" or "post–Masters and Johnson."[3]

The pre–Masters and Johnson therapists recognized, to their credit, that men and women are different in ways that go beyond basic physical differences and that essential masculinity and femininity need to be honored in relationships. However, they lacked information about the physical dynamics of sex and often promoted the erroneous assumption that men were born knowing how to function properly and satisfy their partners. If by chance men didn't know how, they were dismissed as inadequate.

Women were also expected to be orgasmic, again without any training; if they were not, they were labeled as frigid. Ironically, the portrayal of romantic love at that time was consistent with the experience of few people and at odds with the reality of most. Passion and sexual prowess went hand in hand, naturally. People assumed that a "real" man would know how to make love masterfully once he passed through puberty and that a "real" woman could climax on cue—but no one really knew what to do if that wasn't so. Not that the professionals were honest about this. Can you imagine a doctor of the time telling a sexually frustrated couple, "I'm sorry, but we don't know much more than you. Hang in there, folks, and keep trying until we figure it out?" But that is what was happening, and it left no options for men who felt "inadequate" and women who were labeled "frigid." People who experience sexual difficulties—and that's a large population—are much more fortunate today.

What We Lost in the Scientific Era of Sexuality

After *Human Sexual Response*, sex therapists got a better handle on the physiology of lovemaking but, along with the culture at large, they lost a clear sense of the differences between men and women. Some of this had to do with the post–Masters and Johnson stance that idle and unscientific theory was now passé. This group gave little credence to analytical insight or even common folk wisdom. They were much less prone to analyzing why people developed sexual difficulties and more inclined to prescribe practical remedies. The predominant message became "Let us teach you what works, not why," and the public soon embraced this "magic pill" approach. So, as soon as the interventions became available, therapists began to teach men how to reverse premature ejaculation and women how to get past vaginismus (vaginal spasming and closure that makes intercourse very difficult or even impossible). Since therapists didn't know how to "teach" simultaneous orgasm, they ignored it or gave it bad press.

It is not just we who make such statements. Referring to female orgasm during intercourse, respected author and researcher Dr. John Perry has theorized that one of the primary reasons many women do not orgasm during intercourse often or readily is because sexologists incorrectly stated that it doesn't happen.[4]

The other thing lost during this more practical age was the appreciation of gender-based differences. Differences were blurred in the upheaval brought on by the woman's movement and men's subsequent confusion about their identity and roles. The push for equality in personal and social relationships has been absolutely necessary, but the "unisex" culture that emerged in the 1960s and 1970s, with unisex haircuts and clothing and the philosophy that men and women were essentially alike, took the spark out of relationships. Sexual electricity between a man and a woman depends on these differences, on bringing together the two aspects of gender to experience their wholeness through union. People are like battery-powered machines: you have to put the positive and negative poles at variance with each other before they generate the energy to turn on.

In addition to dampening the fire in a lot of sexual relationships, unisex culture frustrates basic human needs. As we've said before, men have a specific set of needs that must be satisfied for them to feel fulfilled as masculine beings. Women have a different set of needs to be fulfilled for them to feel complete as feminine beings. When these needs are not acknowledged and honored, men and women feel alienated from themselves and each other. When these needs are met, each person feels affirmed as an individual, and the union is strengthened.

The science of sexuality for our age needs to both acknowledge gender-specific psychosocial needs *and* embrace the practical. Couples who want to make their intimate relationship the very best it can be must do this on a personal level. We have found over the years that the way to build the best and strongest foundation for fulfilling intimacy is to acknowledge and honor gender differences in your partnership and work to develop joint lovemaking skills. As you set out on this sexual voyage, don't let the official pronouncements of the "sexperts" hold you back. There remains a lot that the so-called experts don't know. We hope—and believe—that it is only a matter of time before sex therapists as a whole define simultaneous orgasm as *one possible outcome of a healthy and enjoyable sexual union; a skill easily learned by couples who want to add this delight to their repertoire.*

Now *that* is a definition worth remembering.

Anita on "Sex Education Today"

As a culture, our attitudes about sexuality are contradictory. When former Surgeon General Jocelyn Elders said that perhaps we should teach masturbation to our children, there was a ridiculous uproar. I thought she was right on. An adolescent who is aware of his or her sexual feelings and who is taught how to act on them responsibly won't get caught off guard in the dating and sexual exploration of those hellacious teenage years.

Encouraging reflection and thoughtfulness about sexuality is infinitely better than the shame messages we continue to push on our children. Messages such as "Don't touch yourself there," "Wait until you are married to have sex," and "All boys want is one thing" teach shame and encourage the gender war. Most children will masturbate—you did, didn't you? It is perfectly natural, and it happens in all cultures. It would be much better for our children to come to know themselves sexually without the baggage we have accumulated.

I have learned from the questionnaires we give to clients that almost everyone masturbated in childhood and almost everyone felt guilty and ashamed about it. Why not give your child the gift of positive, self-affirming information about sexuality? Keep in mind that this is not the same as being permissive. You can help your children recognize their sexual feelings without shame, and you can also help them understand that real self-love dictates they stop and carefully consider whether to follow through on sexual impulses.

If this seems too radical or difficult for you, imagine how your sexual life might be different today if your parents had been able to do this for you.

Climaxing Couples in Popular Literature

Despite the lack of enthusiasm for simultaneous orgasm among the sexperts, the simultaneous orgasm—and our desire for it—has not disappeared. To see where it has been hiding, look at current popular literature. Pick up a novel by Tom Robbins or Anne Rice, or a dime-store romance or two. You will be challenged to find one where the hero and heroine don't come together in a grand and rapturous simultaneous orgasm.

If you share the common belief that women are the only ones who get misty-eyed about climaxing together, check out Nancy Friday's bestseller, *Men in Love: Men's Sexual Fantasies: The Triumph of Love over Rage*. Men fantasize about simultaneous orgasms, too. For one man, the perfect dalliance on a country road draws to a close like this:

Then like bolts of lightning from deep within my guts, came the hot cum coursing through my aching cock and melting her. Her legs wrapped around my hips like a vise and she screamed and sank her teeth into my shoulder. After a long time, I rolled off her and she came to me and pressed her warm wet body against me and we slept.

We want to emphasize that both women *and* men long for this kind of sexual bonding. It is not the romantic fantasy of just one gender, nor can it be suppressed. To remind you of the delicious possibility and variations on this desire, the following are a few more accounts of how couples come together. They all speak to the passion and the possibility that make simultaneous orgasm happen.

As your first "assignment" in this book, read through these accounts and open your mind to what simultaneous orgasm might be like for you, especially if you have never experienced it. Give yourself permission to reread appealing passages again. If you are inspired, seek out these books or other inspiring erotica.

A Smorgasbord of Simultaneous Orgasms in Popular Literature

It makes a vast amount of difference to a man, whether or not his partner is prepared for the final act, for though orgasm may be attained while a woman remains comparatively cold, it can yield nothing like the highest pleasure. That can only come when two people who love, both fully aroused, achieve their culmination, at the same moment—or almost the same moment. The selfish man who does not bother whether his wife is ready for the final act or not, is, like so many selfish creatures, just a fool. His selfishness loses him much joy.

—Eustace Chesser, M.D., *Love Without Fear: How to Achieve Sex Happiness in Marriage* (New York: Signet Books, 1947)

But still the main dish is loving, unselfconscious intercourse—long, frequent, varied, ending with both parties satisfied but not so full they can't face another light course, and another meal in a few hours. The pièce de résistance is the good old face-to-face matrimonial, the finishing off position, with mutual orgasm, and starting with a full day or night of ordinary tenderness.

—Alex Comfort, *The Joy of Sex* (London: Modsets Securities Limited, 1972)

It began with a single voluntary spasm of the engorged outer third of her vagina, at which point she knew that a full orgasm was inevitable. As she cried out that she could wait no longer, a warm, melting sensation spread from her pelvis, suffusing through her entire body, and within seconds she was overwhelmed by powerful vaginal and pelvic contractions, closely synchronized with Ted's. As her body pulsed and rippled deep inside, her cries joined those of her husband. It was a sound for which our language has no adequate words.

—George Leonard, *The End of Sex: Erotic Love After the Sexual Revolution* (New York: Putnam/Tarcher, 1983)

She moved quicker to bring the climax, and when he saw this, he hastened his motions inside of her and excited her to come with him, with words, with his hands caressing her, and finally with his mouth soldered to hers, so that the tongues moved in the same rhythm as the womb and penis, and the climax was spreading between her mouth and her sex, in crosscurrents of increasing pleasure, until she cried out, half sob and half laughter, from the overflow of joy through her body.

—Anaïs Nin, *Delta of Venus* (New York: Harcourt Brace, 1977)

She felt the soft bud of him within her stirring, and strange rhythms flushing up into her with a strange rhythmic growing motion,

swelling and swelling till it filled all her cleaving consciousness, and then began again the unspeakable motion that was not really motion, but pure deepening whirlpools of sensation swirling deeper and deeper through all of her tissue and consciousness, till she was one perfect concentric fluid of feeling, and she lay there crying in unconscious inarticulate cries. . . . "We came off together that time," he said. "It's good when it's like that. Most folks live their lives through and they never know it," he said, rather dreamily. "Don't people often come off together?" she asked with naive curiosity. "A good many of them never. You can see by the raw look of them."
—D. H. Lawrence, *Lady Chatterly's Lover*
(New York: Grove Press, 1969)

She closed her eyes, waiting, waiting, waiting and finally, they began to move together in a point, in counterpoint, in harmony again, a symphonic swelling into a hush and then breaking free, a string melody, a single, ever changing note soaring against the silence . . . up and up, aching, intense, sweet like the curves of her breast, the curve of her cheek, the cling of her mouth on his, of her body on his. And then, almost too late, the note broke, resolved, a shatter, a shimmer of sound and he broke with it, with her, dissolving into her, into elusive hidden essence of her song.
—Francesca Ross, "Wedding Night," in *Fever: Sensual Stories by Women Writers* (New York: HarperCollins, 1994)

He rolled over onto me, and rode me in turn, leaning on his hand so as not to crush me. His balls rubbed against my buttocks, at the entry to my vagina, his hard cock filled me, slid and slid along my deep walls, I dug my nails into his buttocks, he breathed more heavily. . . . We came together, on and on, our fluids mingled, our groans mingled, coming from further in the throat, the depths of our chests, sounds alien to the human voice.
—Alina Reyes, "The Butcher," in *The Mammoth Book of Erotica* (New York: Caroll and Graf, 1994)

> And then he drove into her that thick sex she had desired from the first instant she had seen it. His thrusts were brutal, strong, as if he too, were overcome with denied passion. Her aching sex was filled, her tight nipples throbbing, and she snapped his hips, lifting him as she had lifted the Prince, feeling him fill her, pinion her.
>
> At last she rose up crying out in her relief and she felt him come with a last driving motion. Hot fluids filled her and she lay back, gasping.
>
> She lay against his chest. He cradled her, rocked her, never stopped kissing her.
>
> —Anne Rice, *The Claim of Sleeping Beauty*
> (New York: Penguin Group, 1983)

Notes

1. E. Eichel and P. Nobile, *The Perfect Fit* (New York: Signet Books, 1993), 156.
2. J. Reinisch, *The Kinsey Institute New Report on Sex* (New York: St. Martin's Press, 1990), 127.
3. These periods could also be called the Analytical/Behavioral eras, the Freud/Skinner eras, or the Nature/Nurture eras.
4. Eichel and Nobile, *The Perfect Fit*, 124.

Chapter 3
It's Stupendous...Cosmic... and Within Your Grasp

They can because they think they can.

—Virgil, *The Aeneid*

So, who are you going to believe? The naysayers in the academic sex therapy community or original minds like George Leonard, Anaïs Nin, D. H. Lawrence, Tom Robbins, and Anne Rice? We know, it's a bit like asking whether you would rather dine on day-old bologna or prime rib, but you've got to make the choice—because believing is half the battle.

Here is what we believe: *You can have it.* You and your sweetheart can learn to summon the magic of simultaneous orgasm anytime you find yourselves in the mood. It is a matter of learning a certain set of sensual and physical skills, embracing the mindset, and bringing them together. We say this with complete confidence because we have taught scores of people over the years to do just this. Many clients have come to us because they were having troubles with basic sex, and we were able to help them have simultaneous orgasms regularly. If the basics are already good for you, you are just that much closer to savoring simultaneous delights.

What are the requisite skills? First and foremost, the ability to relax deeply and let go of all distractions during sex. This will free you to be completely attentive to what you're doing and to be receptive to sexual pleasure.

If you are seeking simultaneous orgasm during traditional face-to-face lovemaking, both of you will reach orgasm as a result of stimulation from the other. If the woman can climax by stimulating her clitoris during intercourse, she can enjoy simultaneous orgasm with her partner. If she gets excited quickly, she needs to be able to modulate her arousal. If the man can sustain his erection and modulate his arousal without withdrawing his penis from his partner, he will be able to control his climax. We teach techniques, called "peaking" and "plateauing," that will help you pace yourself so that you can enjoy making love as long as you want to. When you're ready to let yourself be carried over the edge, and you sense your partner is just about there, you need to know how to "trigger" and "hover," so you can help your partner reach the orgasmic threshold when you do.

Don't worry if you don't have any of these skills right now. We've had tremendous success over the years helping people overcome common sexual difficulties to achieve their full sexual potential. Don't let problems such as inorgasmia, premature ejaculation, or erection difficulties hold you back. The next three chapters will show you how to master the basics of sensual touch, and you'll move on to the more advanced techniques of simultaneous orgasm from there. You have every reason to be confident. The step-by-step learning program we've designed has been tested and refined in our clinic for over two decades. We can even help you master multiple orgasms, so you can bring all that you've learned together in a lovemaking extravaganza with multiple mutual orgasms. Now *that* can be spectacular!

All you need is the commitment to learn, the willingness to try the exercises we suggest, the ability to stay with a process until you have mastered it, and some patience and time. And you both need to be motivated. The whole spirit of simultaneous orgasm calls for a mutual eagerness and desire for one.

Be aware, too, that simultaneous orgasm is an emotionally intense experience that you may not want to share with just anyone. Some individuals find the whole idea very scary. Bonding through simultaneous orgasm is not purely physical. It is the mutual exchange of a "me-ness" for an "us-ness," and that is a scarier and more sensitive experience. For example, a major benefit of simultaneous orgasm for some couples is the shared desire and tendency to curl up and sleep in each other's arms afterward, instead of rolling over alone to sleep. This indicates the persistence of the togetherness they have achieved. Without trust, mutual regard for each other, and respect, this level of intimacy may not be reachable.

But if you share those qualities, you may find yourselves enjoying simultaneous orgasm even before you get through all the exercises. Your intention and belief may be enough to take you there. Sex therapist Edward Eichel taught couples a simple intercourse-positioning technique, called the coital alignment technique (CAT), during a study undertaken by the Human Sexuality Program of New York University. The women and men who mastered the technique reported later that they experienced simultaneous orgasm about one-third of the time. That's pretty good, given the fact that Eichel never intended to teach couples how to have a simultaneous orgasm. We do, and our approach is much more thorough. So the results can approach 100 percent if you give it your best effort.

Incidentally, simultaneous orgasm isn't only for the young. In fact, aging can make the experience of simultaneous orgasm even better. With age comes maturity and a greater capacity for intimacy. Given the fact that the refractory period (the time it takes for a man to regain his erection) is longer for older men, the motivation to make each climax special is greater, too.

Bringing New Life into Your Lovemaking

A little earlier we listed the skills necessary to achieve a simultaneous orgasm. But there is more to it than technique. Sexual union is made from your energy, excitement, and of course, your love. Sometimes couples find that although they can bring all that to the bedroom, they can't find their rhythm together. That is because part of their sexual energy is stuck in the past and most of their attention is focused on what they want to happen instead of what is happening. The essence of sexual pleasure is in the moment, in each kiss and caress.

We would like to share two effective exercises that will help you identify the essence of your sexual sensibility and focus solely on the moment. The first exercise, to be done alone, is a visualization designed to liberate your adolescent sexual energy. The second, a two-part exercise will help you ground that energy in the present. It will show you, as a couple, how to bring all of your awareness into the moment. By combining these two, you will be bringing everything you've got into the act!

For many of us, the charge of erotic impulses starts to die almost as soon as we become aware of sexuality. We feel the flush of sexual vitality only to meet with disapproval, rejection, or humiliation. In response, we shut down. Each time we shut down, we have that much less of ourselves to bring to our partners. And we don't feel as much pleasure as we could because the intensity of pleasure depends on our energy levels. Fortunately, we can restore that vitality by going back into the past to retrieve it. That is not as difficult as it sounds—it just takes a little imagination, a little will, and some quiet time.

♀ Exercise ♂
Exploring Your Adolescent Sexuality: It's Better the Second Time Around!

If no one ever gave you permission to explore your body—or to enjoy it— we would like to give it to you now. Take this journey alone first, and then, when it is comfortable for you, make it together with your partner. Think of it as an opportunity to start afresh, just like when you first became lovers.

What was it like when your sexuality first blossomed? What attracted you? What scared you? What did you desire? Did anyone prepare you for what was happening? Would it have been better if there was someone you could trust to take you by the hand and guide you? Now you have the opportunity to do that for yourself. This can be exciting and very healing. This exercise combines your raw teenage energy and your adult know-how through visualization and self-touch.

Before You Begin Choose a room where you will have complete privacy and won't be disturbed for thirty minutes to an hour. Take the phone off the hook and turn off anything that could distract you. Sit in a chair or lie down, loosen any tight clothing or jewelry, and get comfortable.

When You Are Ready You may find it convenient to prerecord the following visualization exercise and play it back when you wish. In fact, you may wish to prerecord many of the exercises in this book if listening to them, rather than rereading them, helps you concentrate.

Focus your attention on your breathing and recognize how easily it produces a deep, gentle relaxation. Let your body "breathe itself" according to its own natural rhythm: slowly, easily, deeply. Let your eyes close and take a "signal breath" to begin the relaxation.

A signal breath is a special message that tells your body you are ready to enter a deep state of relaxation. To take a signal breath, breathe in sharply through your nose (if you can) and exhale fully through your mouth. You may notice a kind of tingling when you take a signal breath. Whatever you feel is your body's way of acknowledging the experience of relaxation, comfort, and peace.

Visualization Concentrate your attention on your breathing. Imagine a ball of pure energy or white light that begins in your lower abdomen. As you inhale, it rises up the front of your body to your forehead. As you exhale, it moves down your spine and legs into the ground. Visualize this ball of energy or light as it travels up the front of your body to your forehead with your inhalation, and as you exhale, it goes down your spine, down your legs, and into the ground.

Circulate this ball of energy for a few minutes, allowing it to move you into a deeper state of relaxation and comfort. Each time you inhale and exhale, you may be surprised to find yourself twice as relaxed as you were a moment before—twice as comfortable, twice as peaceful. With each breath, every fiber of your body eases some more. All the tightness, tension, pain, or discomfort drains down your spine, through your legs, and into the ground, while the pure, radiant energy circulates around.

(Pause here for a few minutes to repeat the breathing cycle.)

As you relax, let your mind go to a place that your teenage self would have found stimulating yet safe. When you get there, what do you see, hear, smell? What time of day is it? Notice where you are and what you are doing.

Slowly conjure an image of your adolescent self at the point when you first felt your sexuality emerge. If you can't form a specific image, make one up.

Take time to visualize your teen self clearly. Notice the details. What do you look like? How is your hair styled? What clothes are you wearing? How are you feeling? Absorb as much as you can.

Now, flow back into your adult self and introduce yourself to your teen. How do you feel toward your teen, and how does she or he feel toward you? Is your teen wary? If so, there may be a good reason.

Explain to your teen that you want to learn all you can about yourself at that age. Let your teen know you won't be judgmental; you want to be friends. At this point, spend some time together and just "hang out." Your goal here is to establish trust between who you are now and who you were at the discovery of your sexuality. Stay with this until you feel this trust.

When trust is established, you can go deeper: Ask your inner teen how she or he feels about her (his) body. Really listen to your teen's response. If feelings of shame or inadequacy come up, talk about it. This is your opportunity to reassure your teenage self that there is no reason to be ashamed of awakening sexuality. A sexually mature body is something to be proud of. Take as much time as is necessary to help your teen understand this.

You might also consider whether you have any wisdom to pass on. You may want to talk about self-love or self-acceptance, independence, or reassurance. Whatever you share, phrase it in a nonjudgmental way.

Consider talking to your teen about masturbation. Most adolescents feel such guilt and shame about sexual touch that, rather than enjoy masturbation, they rush through it as quickly as they can. Help assuage those feelings by explaining that masturbation is the best way to learn about one's body and that it will support a healthy sex life with a future partner.

Ask your teenage self if she or he would like to try masturbating now without shame or guilt. If this still feels scary, discuss why and reassure your teen that she or he is safe. If this is still uncomfortable, skip to the end of the exercise for now.

Self-Touch If your teen is interested in masturbating, make sure you have complete privacy and won't be interrupted. Suggest that your teenager masturbate in the nude and explore his or her entire body. Would he or she like to watch in the mirror, as a partner might see him (her), or lie down? Although you may have suggestions, let your teen choose what feels best.

When ready, visualize the two of you merging together to become one. This way, you both can experience the joy of self-pleasuring.

Take off your clothes slowly and teasingly, just as you might if a lover were watching. Explore your body with your hands and eyes, drawing up the same sense of wonder you had as a teen. Feel all the changes your body has gone through and how good it feels to be touched in so many different places. You may want to use a body oil or lotion, or simply your fingertips—whatever feels good.

Men, if you normally stroke your penis and ignore the rest of your body, this time slow down and discover new erogenous zones. Women, if you normally use a vibrator to bring yourself to orgasm, set it aside. This is a time for exploration.

Stroke your underarms, hips, abdomen, and the insides of your thighs. If you find yourself wanting to go immediately to your genitals, feel the excitement of waiting build while you explore the rest of your body.

Find out if your nipples are sensitive. Men often don't realize how much pleasure and stimulation they can receive from having their nipples caressed. Women may be used to touching only their nipples. Try cupping a breast in your hand and squeezing, or lightly kneading your breasts all over, and then stroking your nipples. Try to recapture the excitement of doing this as a teen, when your breasts were "brand new."

If any embarrassment comes up for your teenage self, talk about it, let him or her know you understand, and explain how important feeling connected to one's own body is to having a great sex life with a partner. You could even mention how much of a turn-on this might be for a partner in years to come.

Masturbation When you feel "warmed up," begin to explore your genitals. Men, remember how catching the almost imperceptible outline of a nipple on the girl who sat across from you in math class made your penis stiffen with curiosity and excitement? As you touch yourself now, reconnect with that youthful exuberance. Use your other hand to massage your testicles or caress your anus, to see what other sensations might add to your experience. If your nipples are sensitive, you may want to stimulate them while you stroke your penis.

Women, remember the thrill of first touching your clitoris or having it touched for the first time by someone else, how the waves of pleasure rolled through your entire body? How do you best like your clitoris to be touched? Experiment with different strokes, using your other hand to explore the inside of your vagina, touch your breasts, or caress any area of your body that feels pleasurable.

While you explore, don't forget those teenage fantasies—whether they were of your favorite rock star or your best friend's older sibling. This time, with no parents in the next room, you can really let yourself go. You can even imagine your partner watching you as a teenager exploring your body with eagerness and enthusiasm.

Feelings and Emotions If any shame-related thoughts intrude during self-touch and masturbation, remember that exploring your sexuality is a positive, healing thing to do for yourself. Your sexuality is part of your life force; connecting to it helps you to be more present and alive. It enables you to reach out for intimacy with a partner. How can energy, love, and intimacy be bad?

If feelings of shame persist, no matter how much you reassure your teen (and yourself), it might be helpful to discuss them with a therapist who specializes in sexuality, or with your current therapist. Some of us need more time than others to work through issues of shame and guilt that often surround sexuality. The important thing is that you do it. Remember, you have the right to enjoy your sexuality.

You may or may not choose to bring yourself to orgasm during this exercise. That is entirely your choice. Do not feel pressured or restrained.

When you are finished with the exercise, if there is more you would like to explore, make arrangements to get together with your teen self again. If you make a date, be sure not to break it. Breaking a date betrays trust. You want to be able to trust yourself, to open yourself fully. Then say good-bye.

After you have done that, take a signal breath to let your body know you are ending the exercise (breathe in sharply through your nose; exhale fully through your mouth). Slowly close and open your eyes, and come back to the present moment.

After the Exercise How was that for you? Take a moment to reflect on what you learned about yourself. Does your inner teen need more of your time? Is there anything you need to do for yourself during the week to keep that connection alive? Ask yourself: what will it take to feel as aware and electric now as I was back then? How can I make space for that in my life right now? Take some time to draw a picture or write about this experience in a journal.

♀ Exercise ♂
Exploring Your Adolescent Sexuality as a Couple: Part One

After you and your partner have each done the Adolescent Sexuality exercise alone at least once, set aside time to do the following exercise together. Pick a time when there is peace between you; you need to feel very safe so that you can really play with this. If you have children, make arrangements for them to be out of the house or asleep so that you won't be interrupted.

We suggest you read the exercise into a tape recorder, then play the tape back during the exercise, so that you can relax and focus on each other during the exercise. In some sections, you will pause for a short time. If you like, record music that you both enjoy during the pauses. You may want to choose music from the era when you were a teen. If you are very different ages, choose something you both enjoy and find sexy. Although you are together, this exercise should be done individually.

Before You Begin Prepare yourselves together as you did separately for the previous exercise.

Visualization Again, imagine the ball of energy or light as it travels up the front of your body when you inhale, and down your spine, down your legs, and into the ground as you exhale. Circulate this ball of energy for a few minutes. Allow its circulation to move you into a deeper state of relaxation and comfort. Each time you inhale and exhale, you may find yourself twice as relaxed as you were a moment before—twice as comfortable, twice as peaceful. With each breath, every cell of your body eases the tightness, tension, pain, or discomfort in your body, drains it down your spine, down your legs, and into the ground. Let this energy circulate around.

(Pause here for a few moments to repeat the breathing cycle.)

As you relax, close your eyes and imagine you and your partner in a fabulous, intimate setting. It is a place where you can explore your adolescent sexuality together. Look around this wonderland. What do you see? Take some time here to really get to know this place: what it looks like, what it feels like, and how you feel in it.

(Pause for up to two minutes.)

Allow an image to form of your adolescent self. Is it the same image as in the previous exercise? If so, say hello and reintroduce yourself. If the image is different, get to know that teen self.

Now it's time to meet your partner's adolescent self. Begin by imagining your partner as a teenager. You may have seen photos of your partner, or you might even have known him or her at this age. If not, you can make it up. As the image comes into focus, notice the details that emerge. What color is your partner's hair? How tall is he or she? What is your partner wearing? A fringed leather jacket? A poodle skirt and bobby socks? A letterman's jacket?

Take a really good look. Take a walk around your partner's adolescent self. When you are ready, introduce yourself. See what it feels like to be with your partner as a teenager.

(Pause for a few minutes to visualize your partner as a teenager.)

Tell your partner how much you love him or her, especially as you get to know each other in this new way. Say how turned on you are right now. In your mind, begin a fun and sensual "make out" session.

Remember what it was like to make out with all your clothes on, feeling the excitement and anticipation only a teenager feels. Remember what it was like to eagerly explore another person for the very first time.

(Pause for at least five minutes to imagine your makeout session.)

Imagine slowly undressing each other. Whether or not you knew your partner at this age (and most of you probably did not), imagine what it might have felt and looked like to do this—the sense of wonder and awe you might have felt.

In your mind, take time to discover your partner's body. If you are a man, you might imagine seeing and touching her breasts for the very first time, feeling the excitement of a sixteen-year-old boy doing it. Imagine seeing her vagina up close for the very first time, parting her lips, discovering her clitoris. If you are a woman, imagine seeing your partner naked as an adolescent, as the first naked man you have seen in real life. Touch him everywhere, allowing your curiosity to lead you. Remember the excitement you felt feeling a penis become erect in your hand for the very first time.

As you continue your teenage exploration of one another, remember that there is nothing shameful or wrong about doing so. As you learned when you explored your own body, sexuality is both a life force and a way to express deep love for yourself and your partner.

(Pause for five to ten minutes to explore and discover your partner's teenage body.)

Let your teenage partner know that you love him or her. Tell your partner that you honor and respect him or her, too. Make a date to do this again very soon.

After the Exercise Take a signal breath, to signal that the exercise is over. When you are ready, open your eyes and hug your partner. Look at each other without speaking and reflect on what you experienced. Before talking, take a minute to write about what you experienced, or use crayons or colored pencils to capture your feelings in color. Then, if you are comfortable, share your experience with your partner. Consider having a few more "encounter" sessions before having sex, so you can let the charge build before you let yourself act on those feelings.

♀ Exercise ♂
Exploring Your Adolescent Sexuality as a Couple: Part Two

After you have practiced Part One of this exercise several times, try it in real life. Be prepared to delight in the adolescent drives and desires you and your partner now embody.

Before You Begin Prepare an intimate space in your home, or if you can, spend a night in an intimate hotel or romantic vacation spot. You may wish to light candles and have soft music playing in the background. You could have silk sheets and incense. The important thing is to create the kind of ambiance you will both luxuriate in and enjoy.

When you do the exercise this time, you may wish to play the tape of the previous exercise, but this time *act* on your feelings.

When You Are Ready After a few minutes of deep breathing to relax and center yourselves, take a signal breath to begin the exercise.

Imagine each other as adolescents. Really look for that young, innocent part of one another. Bring a youthful sense of joy and wonder to your encounter. Then gaze at each other, take that first tentative kiss, and make out as your sexual energy builds.

Feel each other's nipples and genitals through clothing, and relish that teenage sense of uncertainty, anticipation, and thrill. Slowly undress one another, and joyfully, sensuously, explore each other's bodies. Be respectful of your partner's feelings, and check in with your partner about what she or he is experiencing. Try not to have any expectations.

Do this exercise for fifteen minutes. When the time is up, take a signal breath to let your body know that you are finished. Give each other a hug.

After the Exercise Take a few minutes to talk about the experience of this exercise. There is no right or wrong way to do this. If the experience seems awkward at first, consider trying it again another time. You can change the setting to more fully evoke the experience. For example, lay a blanket down in the woods at twilight, stay downstairs in the living room after your "parents" (or the kids) have gone to bed, or find a safe place to "park." Remember how much trouble you used to go to as a teenager so you could be alone with your sweetheart? Use that same romantic ingenuity to get those feelings stirring again.

• • •

You may have to revisit your adolescent self alone (or together) a number of times to get in touch with your basic, unfettered sexual energy, but it's worth it. You are unlikely to find a better source of natural sexual energy than in your own teenage self.

After getting back in touch with your adolescent energies, take that feeling of being perpetually turned on and let it cycle through your adult body in everyday life. Breathe it through your limbs. Feel alive in your senses. Allow the secret of it to be your constant companion, clinging close as a cloud of fragrance. Stop during the day, when responsibilities begin to pile up, and take a moment to focus on it. Feel it as a source of power inside you, glowing through your skin. Let yourself smile—you know you've got something worth sharing.

Life together can get really good when you can integrate the raw sexual energy of adolescence with a childlike, innocent delight in sensuality. Although it may seem like going backwards, your intimate life together can take a huge step forward when you make the time to explore each other the way children do, just for the delight of it. In your day-to-day life, take the time to touch each other without desire or pressure to "go all the way." Sex therapists call this nondemand interaction, and children do this all the time. Rediscover your delight in the nonsexual aspects of your physical relationship and each other's bodies.

Savoring Your Sensuality: The Sensate Focus Approach

Sensuality feeds another kind of hunger, a desire for sexual experience that we were meant to feel and to take pleasure in. If we weren't, why would our sense be so keen? We may not have a hawk's sharp eyesight or a dog's uncanny sense of smell, but our own abilities are pretty impressive. For instance, we can feel on our fingertips or on our faces a pressure that depresses the skin by only 1/25,000 of an inch. We can see a candle flame thirty miles away on a clear night. We can smell one drop of perfume diffused through a three-bedroom apartment. Our taste buds are developed enough to detect 1/25 of an ounce of salt diluted by 500 quarts of water. Pretty amazing, isn't it?

This same acuity allows us to feel the subtlest nuances in sensation when a lover is near. So, becoming more sensual together will do more for your relationship than simply increase sexual satisfaction. Sensuality involves a deeper level of intimacy than sexuality.

Take kissing, for instance. It is sensual and extremely intimate. Prostitutes who will engage in a number of sex acts often draw the line at kissing, because it is so personal; they can have intercourse and remain emotionally detached, but kissing takes sex to another level.

Not just sex, but anything you do together can be sensual, as long as you pay attention with your mind and your senses. The next time you sit down to eat, just the two of you, consider what it would be like to enjoy the meal with your senses enhanced. Notice the color and texture of the food. Focus on the taste and the odors. Listen for sounds: the clinking of glasses, the plate being placed on the table. Watch the expressions change on your partner's face, as if in slow motion. Let your thoughts slow down and your senses sharpen.

Remember how keen your senses were when you first fell in love? You were acutely aware of everything about your partner: the smell of his skin or of her hair, the feeling of her fingertips on your arm, and the anticipation of your fingertips as they traveled down his body. This is the level of sensitivity you need to cultivate again, even if it has been dulled over many years. This sensuality will allow your lovemaking to set its own agenda, uniquely appropriate to the moment, instead of settling into a pattern of what you always do. When you remove the patterns, there's room for something unexpected to happen, something that's never happened before—like simultaneous orgasm.

Developing physical relaxation and heightened sensual awareness will make you more orgasmic and more in control of your sexual response. Sensate focus activities (the array of behaviorally oriented exercises pioneered by Masters and Johnson) are an excellent, erotic way to learn how to do this. They are also particularly good for men with premature ejaculation or erection difficulties and for women who have difficulty reaching orgasm. Sensate focus techniques heighten your arousal, increase your relaxation, and most important, take the pressure off.

There are three "rules" to follow when doing sensate focus. The first is: *Focus on your sensations.* The second is: *Keep your focus in the here and now, releasing all extraneous thoughts.* The third is: *Enjoy yourself without having any expectations of yourself or your partner.*

You will find these three rules incredibly freeing—and they are also essential ingredients for good sex.

The following exercise, called the back caress, is one we recommend to couples to help them get back in touch with their sensuality. It is more sensual, less sexual, and easy to start out with. If you were to begin with the front of each other's bodies, you would naturally include the genitals and could easily slip into old patterns. Learning how to be sensual is the point of this exercise.

♀ Exercise ♂
The Back Caress

Before You Begin Set aside at least an hour when you can be together without distractions. Make sure the room is warm and comfortable. Begin by undressing, then lie down together and cuddle. You can hold each other in a face-to-face embrace or lie back-to-front in the comforting "spoon" position. Decide which of you will be the "active" partner first. The active partner initiates touching. You will switch roles after twenty minutes. This caress is non-verbal.

When You Are Ready The active partner spends twenty minutes caressing the other's back. Caressing is a lighter touch than massage. It is a stroke, soft and smooth, or light and feathery. When you are the active partner, touch for your own pleasure, but change your stroke if your partner tells you he or she doesn't like what you're doing. Don't touch with the intention of creating arousal, and don't focus on traditionally sexual or erogenous areas. Stay in the moment, simply enjoying the contact and the closeness.

Experiment with using your arms, face, chest, legs, and feet to caress your partner's back. Make full-body contact by lying down on your partner. Allow your love to flow through your touch.

When you are the passive partner, don't give feedback unless your partner is doing something that is uncomfortable. If you like what you feel, stay with the sensations.

Whether you are active or passive, always remember and practice the three golden rules described above. If your mind should wander, do not feel badly. The tendency to wander is quite common, but easily overcome. Whenever you wander, simply refocus your attention on the physical feelings you are having. You may need to do this many times until it happens spontaneously, but with enough practice it will.

After twenty minutes, cuddle again and switch roles. Just let the partner who has been passive now take a turn being active. When you are finished, cuddle some more. You'll probably both feel very relaxed.

• • •

You can do the back caress any time you feel a desire to reconnect physically, without putting any pressure on each other to make something happen or to have sex. It is a wonderful way to unwind after a stressful workday, and it is a great way to relax together and reinitiate your union if one of you has been out of town for some time. The back caress can be a tender experience in and of itself, or it can serve as a prelude to the exercises in the chapters to come.

While it may seem like a long way from the simple back caress to the simultaneous orgasm, it is really the first big step. The degree of relaxation and the ability to focus on sensual process rather than potential sexual result is the key. The parts of you that "know" how to bring your arousal cycles into harmony with each other will have a much easier time of it if you can learn how to stay this relaxed and open with each other now and later, as your sensuality and stimulation become more and more intense.

• • •

As you journey ahead on the pleasure path to simultaneous orgasm, remember to savor each step of your travels. Enjoy the sweet success in every small and sexy accomplishment along the way. Let the exploration be a joyous experience. Before you know it, your cherished goal will be in your command.

Voluptuous Variations on What's to Come

Simultaneous orgasms come in as many varieties as sequential orgasms. They are not limited to face-to-face intercourse. You can bring them about in any intercourse position, for example, in the racy "69" position or while you manually pleasure each other or yourselves. Mutual oral sex and mutual masturbation are a bit more challenging because they are rich with stimulation—both what you give and receive—so it is more difficult to concentrate on your own orgasmic sensations. Some couples, however, find these variations wonderfully satiating.

Within each of these options are even more delicious choices. Men may take pleasure in an ejaculatory orgasm, an orgasm without ejaculation, or multiple orgasms. Ejaculation and orgasm are not the same, as we explain in Chapter 7. Men who are able to have multiple orgasms learn how to separate ejaculation from orgasm, so that they can climax without ejaculating or losing their erections.

Women can delight in a full-body vaginal orgasm, a hot, focused clitoral orgasm, a G-spot orgasm, or a "gusher"—an intense G-spot orgasm accompanied by the release of fluid.

Even with intercourse, simultaneous orgasm isn't limited to orgasms that begin and end at the same time. A woman who is capable of multiple orgasms could begin her orgasmic cycle alone while her partner, through ejaculation control, may allow his own excitement to build until she is midway through her cycle. Alternatively, he may surrender to his climax when hers begins or ends. Many women find that their partner's orgasm triggers their own, and so what begins as a sequential orgasm becomes a simultaneous orgasm.

Given all of these options, you can just imagine the mix-and-match possibilities. You don't have to give up having sex the way you like it just because you'd like to climax together. And you certainly don't have to have it the same way, all the time. On the contrary, you can take the sex you like to greater orgasmic heights. Variety is the spice of life, after all!

Part Two
Learning How

Chapter 4
Before Play: Laying the Groundwork for Great Sex

There is a commitment, however brief; a purity, however threatened; a vulnerability, however concealed; a generosity of spirit, however marbled with need; an honest caring, however singed by lust, that must be present if couplings are to be salubrious and not slow poison.

—Tom Robbins, *Still Life with Woodpecker*

ow often have you grabbed something out of the fridge and eaten it cold, standing up, because you were in a rush or very hungry? It stopped your hunger, but did it satisfy you? A great meal, a truly memorable one, takes careful preparation. Many different ingredients go into the preparation, with attention given to each one.

So it is with great sex. While desire can ignite spontaneously, sex itself is only as good as what you bring to it. Body and soul, mind and emotions all need to be primed and ready. Why bring your lover anything less than the best? Why deny yourself the experience of full sexual vitality?

When you think about it, sex is much more than desire and instinct, nakedness and contact. A lot happens beneath the skin, too. Sex is glandular, vascular, muscular, neural, cognitive, perceptual, biochemical, and electrical. You must have "all systems go," in harmonious interplay, to experience something more than a bumping here and a grinding there.

Desire—that profoundly human creation—generates from all levels of your being. It starts in the innermost self as a hunger, a sense of incompleteness, and a reaching toward that which it believes is fulfillment. You may not be conscious of your sexual appetite until an external stimulus tickles it and brings it to the foreground. Perhaps a shapely stranger brushes by you on the street and something inside of you thinks, "Mmm, would I like . . ." Or maybe you read an erotic passage in a novel, or your lover says something to you in that tone of voice that stirs forces deep and primal.

The flush of desire that stirs within you then is possible because your spirit percolates the sexual impulse through your brain, inspiring it to send commands throughout your body to bring organs and glands into a state of sexual readiness. You might not feel desire if your sexual glands were not functioning properly, releasing precise amounts of estrogen, progesterone, and testosterone into your bloodstream. (Abnormally high levels of estrogen may depress desire, while very high levels of testosterone can throw it into overdrive. What constitutes too high or too low varies from one individual to the next.) The experience of desire also requires a certain sensitivity in the nerves, which translates excitement into physical sensation and sexual arousal. This is the warm, erotic flush you feel in your lover's presence. Your inner hunger for intimacy, your past emotional and sexual history with each other, your physical nearness, and your anticipation of what is to come all play a part in what happens next.

When you look at it this way, it's not hard to see how sexuality engages every aspect of being. It necessarily follows that the best way to prepare for the kind of intimacy that will fulfill you, body and soul, is to nourish and vitalize each of these aspects of you. (Doing so will also develop the magnetism others find so hard to resist, and, as you know, there's nothing quite as delicious as feeling desired by the one you desire.)

How do you create that sexual magnetism? How do you awaken full sexual vitality? The answers are our promise for the pages ahead. In this chapter, we explain the systems of desire and arousal, to help you develop the simple daily habits that will get you there.

The Foundation for Sensational Sex

Five elements are critical for full sexual pleasure: a sense of overall vitality; tone and elasticity in specific pelvic muscles; the ability to switch your attention from thoughts to physical sensations; the ability to relax mind and body deeply, and at will; and the right attitude—an honest acceptance of both your own sexuality and your partner's.

Let's look at each of these elements in turn.

Vitality

It's almost too obvious to mention, but vitality is an absolute prerequisite for great sex. Just ask any athlete. The more physically fit you are, the better you are able to enjoy the physicality of sex. Any activity that stimulates vitality is worth building into your regular schedule. If running keeps you stoked, run. If you enjoy reggae, go out dancing or break out your favorite CDs. If walking in the forest is what brings your senses fully alive, get out your hiking boots. It doesn't matter which activity you choose, just get moving.

Exercise oxygenates the blood and stimulates circulation. Good circulation heightens your skin's sensual receptivity and is necessary to keep an erection robust and a clitoris engorged to the point of orgasm. Exercise builds stamina and increases flexibility, and you'll be thankful for both during a vigorous lovemaking session.

If, on a regular basis, you can exercise to the point of sweating, so much the better. Sweating cleans your blood of toxins and brings a host of benefits: glowing skin, lustrous eyes, and an overall liveliness to your appearance. You've probably noticed that when aerobically fit, you feel better about yourself and more positive about life in general. What you may not know is that feeling really good about yourself is the major component of your overall attractiveness to others.

The foods you eat also contribute to your sense of well-being. A diet of live, whole foods, including plenty of fresh fruits and vegetables and whole grains, nourishes your organs and glands. On the other hand, the wrong foods can devitalize you, making you sluggish and irritable. Certainly it's okay to enjoy an eclair now and then or savor a juicy steak with potatoes swimming in sour cream, but don't make a habit of this if your sex life is important to you. Over time, a diet of high-fat foods may clog the arteries enough to create erection difficulties for men and can make anyone too tired for sex at all. A diet that relies heavily on junk food can dull overall sexual responsiveness. Why spend vital energy processing unhealthy foods when you can spend it on pleasure? Your food choices become even more important as you age, because the body is slower to replenish what has been lost.

It is also important to guard against the stresses of everyday life. If you're going, going, going or thinking, thinking, thinking from the minute the alarm clock goes off until you lay your head back down on the pillow at night, consider how much wear this places on your organs, glands, and body systems. If you don't take regular breaks for your body to rejuvenate, don't be surprised if you begin to feel less sexual and the physical intimacy with your partner falls short of ideal. Over time, if you fail to find the right balance between rest and activity for *you* (it varies from individual to individual), your desire may disappear entirely.

Also, if you live a fairly routine life, always playing it safe instead of taking the risks that bring richness to your life, don't expect your sex to sizzle for very long. Sex never has been and never will be a substitute for full-contact living. Let your life sizzle first, and the sex will follow.

Eat, Drink, and Be Randy

People have experimented with aphrodisiacs throughout the ages, but no particular food, herb, or elixir can substitute for a good, balanced diet. That's because to be in prime sexual condition you've got to feed your brain, muscles, nerves, glands, and sexual organs—and no one substance can do that. To feel really alive in your body and energized for sex, incorporate as many live foods (fresh fruits, vegetables, and sprouts) into your diet as you can. The fresh juices of fruits and vegetables are also excellent. The greater the life energy in the food or beverage, the greater the stimulus to your own life energy.

Also, be sure to drink eight full glasses of pure water each day. Water helps with internal hygiene by flushing out toxins. The cleaner you feel inside, the more sensitive you are to pleasurable stimuli, such as your lover's touch.

> If you think hormonal levels could be affecting you, consider talking to a reproductive endocrinologist who specializes in these matters, or consult a nutritionist, acupuncturist, or other expert health care practitioner. You may have to experiment a bit before you find the nutritional program that's right for you.
>
> If your testosterone levels are low, consider whether you're getting enough animal protein. An article published in *Men's Health* magazine reported that men who eat meat have higher testosterone levels than those who rely on soybeans or other vegetarian protein alternatives. (Meat can be high in estrogens, however, depending on the farming methods.)
>
> If you think your diet could use a tune-up, check out *Love, Sex and Nutrition*, by nutritionist Bernard Jensen (Garden City, NY: Avery Publishing Group, 1988).

Focused Sexual Toning

While sex is by no means limited to the genital area, you can get a lot of bang for your buck, so to speak, by lavishing attention on a few key muscles. The most important is the pubococcygeus (PC) muscle, which connects the pubic bone to the coccyx (or tailbone). This is the muscle that spasms during orgasm in both men and women. Know the one? Try finding it right now. An easy way to identify the muscle is to urinate, and then intentionally start and stop the flow. Men will find that contracting the PC muscle during an erection causes the penis to flick up and down.

There are health as well as sexual benefits to keeping your PC muscle toned. For women, a well-toned PC muscle will help keep urinary and reproductive organs in place as they age, preventing a condition called a prolapsed uterus. It will also help prevent urinary incontinence, a problem common with age. For men, keeping the PC muscle in shape may help prevent problems with the prostate. A toned PC muscle enhances the intensity and duration of orgasms and enables more control over climax.

Everyone should exercise his or her PC muscle every day. It's easy and can be done anywhere, at any time. The hardest thing is simply remembering to do it. Try doing the following PC muscle exercises each day at the same time, so you establish a routine. We find it helpful to combine them with a daily activity, such as brushing your teeth.

The PC Squeeze While keeping all other muscles relaxed (including stomach, legs, and buttocks), squeeze your PC muscle and hold it tight for a full second.

Release it, and then relax for a full second.

Repeat this tighten-relax sequence ten times.

This only takes about twenty seconds—it's so easy and simple. Begin by doing one set of squeezes a day, and work up to three. In a short time, you will notice results. As you feel your PC getting stronger, it will become easier to hold the tension for longer periods of time.

When you feel you've got it down, experiment a little. Do it more rapidly, hold it longer, or try fluttering it. Mix it up: short squeeze, long squeeze, and so on. But beware—don't overdo it. The PC will get sore, like any other unconditioned muscle, and an aching PC is no fun. Take it easy at first; then increase your reps. Happily, about three sets of ten repetitions a day is all that is needed for healthy maintenance.

Pelvic Thrusts and Rolls Pelvic thrusts and rolls are also worth incorporating into your daily routine because of the flexibility they bring. They loosen up the muscles and tendons in your thighs, lower back, and hips, which gives you more energy and less tension when you make love. Most things in our lives—driving, sitting, and so forth—conspire to keep this area of our body locked up tight.

To do thrusts, lie on your back or stand up, and move your pelvis back and forth while keeping the rest of your body still. To do rolls, circle your pelvis as if you were keeping a hula hoop going.

Try doing five minutes of thrusts and five minutes of rolls each day, until you've got them down. Then alternate thrusts and rolls in random, alternating patterns.

• • •

Doing specific stretching exercises aimed at limbering and strengthening the muscles in your inner thighs, thighs, abdomen, and buttocks can also greatly increase your pleasure, because they bring a greater flow of energy to the area. (Remember, energy equals sexual charge.) Underlying cultural attitudes about pleasure have taught many of us to keep these muscles chronically tense, so that we block sensations in the area. This tension is a common response, for instance, when a parent scolds a young child for touching his or her genitals. Wilhelm Reich, a body-oriented psychotherapist who was light-years ahead of his time, observed that Western society is organized around getting people to control their pleasures rather than teaching them how to enjoy them.

If you are serious about freeing yourself sexually, consider treating yourself to a regular course of bodywork. Reichian therapy and bioenergetics, which evolved from Reichian work, are two systems of body-oriented psychotherapy concerned primarily with unblocking sexual energy. If you would like bodywork but are not interested in exploring the psychodynamics of how your muscles got to be so tense, then you might consider acupressure or Swedish massage, which are two other rewarding options.

Sensate Focus: A Concentration of the Senses

The ability to relax your mind and body deeply, at will, is critical if you want to experience optimal physical pleasure. This is true for a number of reasons. One simple reason is that tense muscles "lock in" energy. When making love, you want energy to flow freely and to be available to you so you can move with it and drive the pace of lovemaking—or approximate your lover's pace, as the situation calls for. The more energy available to you, the greater your sense of release and the deeper your pleasure when you climax.

Mental relaxation is also important, because thoughts create tension in the muscles. Thoughts compete with physical sensations for your attention. If your mind or muscles are too tense, the "conservator" in your brain will inhibit or completely shut down your sexual functioning. This can happen even if you very much want to make love but are overanxious about pleasing or impressing your partner. It is just as likely to happen, however, if you are fearful about an unrelated stress, like the possibility that you may be laid off from work. Even non-tension-producing thoughts can distract you from feeling sexual sensation. To understand why this happens, let's look at how the brain and the nervous system work.

Your brain and nervous system essentially have two "settings" each. One is optimal for sexual functioning; the other inhibits it. Nature did this to provide the kind of responses that ensured early human survival.

The more primitive part of the brain, the hind brain, governs primal instincts, base emotions, and sexual behavior. The cortex is the seat of the higher functions of mind, such as abstract thinking, analysis, and logic. Some people refer to these as the "animal" brain and the "thinking" brain.

The animal brain and the thinking brain are in constant communication with each other, and they keep each other in check. For the most part, this system works wonderfully. When one is active, the other hums in the background. For example, when you use your brain to solve abstract equations, the cortex keeps a lid on sexual desire. In fact, it is the job of the cortex to suppress sexual urges when acting on them would be inappropriate.

For those of us who make heavy use of our brain during the work week, the trick is to learn how to let the cortex "idle" so that our animal brain can come out to play when we take a lover to bed. There is a time and a place to surrender to and satisfy those libidinous urges, and it can be disheartening and sexually disappointing if the moment is right but your thinking brain won't quit. Just remember the last time you had an internal monologue about whether or not you were doing a good job satisfying your lover, and you'll know what we mean.

Ideally, when you are making love, you concentrate on the physical sensations the sexual contact creates. Being in the here and now means that you can narrow your awareness to what you are experiencing in this precise place, in this precise moment. Thoughts unrelated to what you are experiencing in the here and now do not enter your mind. You flow with the moment, without making any particular demands on your partner, and in full confidence that your partner has no particular expectations of you, either. This is incredibly freeing and an essential ingredient of good sex. (Sex therapists call this *nondemand interaction*.)

Relaxation of Body and Mind

The brain isn't the only part of you that needs to gear down for great sex. Your nervous system has to be in the right gear as well. There are two branches of the nervous system, and the one that allows for full sexual functioning is called the parasympathetic nervous system. You know this system is operative when your breathing is slow and steady and your muscles are relaxed. This system is active when you feel deeply aroused.

Because modern life doesn't tend to be very relaxing, most of us are more familiar with the other branch of the autonomic nervous system, the sympathetic nervous system. This is the branch that springs into action when you are stressed. Nature created this system to help the body mobilize the energy to either fight or take flight. Where the parasympathetic nervous system may take a few moments to take over, the sympathetic nervous system works very quickly. Within seconds of perceived danger, the eyes dilate, the heart pounds, and breathing and blood pressure increase dramatically. Blood in the body's core speeds to the arms and legs, so they have the energy to move quickly. This has the effect of depressing sexual function, however, since the blood flows out of the engorged genital area toward the limbs.

Unfortunately, this fine-tuned system can get modern men and women in trouble if they are prone to anxiety or are under stress. Internal anxiety, no matter what the cause, can trigger the sympathetic nervous system at inopportune moments. Once it kicks in, you can forget about any gratifying sex. The only way to shift back into parasympathetic mode is to consciously focus on relaxation.

Four techniques are explained below—conscious breathing; grounding; tensing/relaxing; and massage—that can all help you to fully relax. They can be done at any time, and are not necessarily part of your sexual activity. You can use them in any situation where stress reduction is desirable.

Conscious Breathing One of the most effective ways to consciously relax is through slow, deep breathing. When anxious, you tend to breathe shallowly or hold your breath. By making yourself inhale slowly through your nostrils and exhale fully through your mouth, you can consciously bring about relaxation.

If you tend to be anxious often or are going through a stressful period in life, it's a good idea to stop periodically throughout the day and check your breathing. Notice whether it is shallow or deep. Bring your attention into your body and find where you feel tension. See if you can use your breath to help you let go of tension. When you are having sex, it is doubly important to check in with your breathing from time to time, until it becomes second nature.

Grounding Another way to let go of tension and reconnect with your body is to consciously "ground" yourself. This can really help if you often find your thoughts running away with you. To ground yourself, get into a comfortable position. You can either sit or stand, but make sure you feel your feet firmly planted on the ground. Imagine roots extending from your feet deep into the earth. Take a deep breath through your nostrils. Breathe out through your mouth, and imagine you are sending the breath down your legs, out your feet, and through your roots. Use your breath in this way to take relaxing energy into your body and send tension out. Grounding should take no longer than thirty seconds to do, and you can repeat it as often as needed.

Tensing/Relaxing If you have at least twenty minutes to spare, you can achieve a very deep state of relaxation by consciously tensing and then releasing your muscles. If you take a train or bus to work, you can do this unobtrusively on the commute home. It works best, however, if you do this in a private space where you are free from all distractions.

Before you begin, loosen any tight clothing that could prevent you from taking slow, deep belly breaths. Then breathe deeply, taking air in through your nostrils and releasing it through your mouth. When you have released surface tensions in this way, begin to focus on tensing and then relaxing each body part separately. Take a few seconds to tense the part, and then hold the tension for a few seconds before you exhale and release. Let yourself feel how relaxed that body part is before you move on to the next one.

Work from the feet up. Tense and relax your left foot first, and then your right foot. Then do the same with your legs, buttocks, abdomen, hands, arms, chest, neck, and face.

When you are finished, take five deep relaxing breaths. Then compliment yourself on how well you've done. Use your mind to scan your body; if you still feel tension anywhere, tense and relax those areas again until they are at ease.

If this feels too challenging, or you think relaxing music can help, buy an audio tape designed for this purpose. You can find relaxation tapes in mail-order or wellness catalogues, New Age bookstores, and some music stores. If you get professional massages on a regular basis, ask your massage practitioner what she or he recommends. Alternatively, you could make a tape of the relaxation exercise in Chapter 6, page 118, called "Reconnecting with Sexuality, Reawakening Desire: A Guided Imagery Exercise."

Massage Yet another very pleasurable way to keep yourself relaxed and primed for lovemaking is to go for regular massages or, better yet, to exchange them with your lover. Massage is a great way to throw off tension and get breath moving through your body again. It aids circulation, eliminates toxins, and improves muscle tone and function. It can also build trust between lovers. A massage will help you shift from a stressed-out state into one in which you are highly aroused and receptive.

Scheduling a massage before a special date (and you should still make special dates with each other no matter how many years you've been married!) is also a great idea. You'll look better and feel better, and you'll find yourself anticipating the pleasures of the evening ahead. In bed, you'll find that you're more responsive and aroused. Men often find it easier to sustain erection and last as long as they like. Women often find themselves more orgasmic.

The Right Attitude

Up until now, we have focused primarily on the physical elements of sexual pleasure. Exercise, the right diet, and regular relaxation breaks can give you a lot more juice in bed and intensify your pleasure. But the road to full sexual vitality doesn't stop there. You have to put your head in the right place, too. If it is filled with expectations about your partner or pressure on yourself to perform according to a certain ideal, your mind is not receptive to the sexual signals flowing between you and your lover. Simultaneous orgasm requires you to be absorbed in the moment, in your pleasure and the pleasure of your lover. It takes a high degree of attunement.

Attitudes about sex or yourself that are even a little off can get in the way. There is a lot of "pleasure-fear" in the collective American subconscious. We are a nation founded by Puritans, and on top of that contemporary culture pushes a "make it happen now" mindset. Combine the two, and what do you get? Tension and pleasure-numbing fear in the bedroom. Either of these are enough to create a wall between you and your lover. It can take a lot of self-awareness, caring, and mutual support to take that wall down.

To help you start taking down that wall, we want to highlight faulty, often subconscious beliefs that may be getting in your way. Until you bring these to the surface, all efforts and good intentions to improve your sex life may not bear fruit.

Faulty Idea 1: Sex is dirty or shameful, or "Nice girls don't."

Sure, you are too educated and progressive to believe this consciously, but what did your parents tell you? Deborah tells us a funny story about when she was a teenager and a passionate young Hispanic man was courting her. Her uptight Italian-American mother didn't like this but said nothing until one day when mother and daughter were shopping for new underwear. The teenager left her purchase at the checkout counter by mistake, and she didn't realize it until she and her mother were riding down the escalator. Whereupon her mother scolded her, loud enough for everyone else to hear, "Deborah, don't *ever* lose your panties!"

Deborah's story is funny until you consider the underlying message. Many women who come to us for therapy feel shame about their sexuality. It seems to be less of a problem for men, in general, although it can be just as crippling for those it affects. Chapter 6, for women, will deal with the issue of shame more fully, but we mention it here so you can explore together whether this is an issue for either of you.

Resolving any feelings of shame will liberate you to be freer in your lovemaking and more in the moment. It will boost your overall self-esteem, and you will feel the effects in all areas of your life. The terrible thing about feeling shame about having sexual feelings is that we all have sexual feelings—in fact, they are rooted in our very physiology.

Faulty Idea 2: It's my job to bring my partner to orgasm, or "A real man knows how to make her come."

As we said in Chapter 2, about 50 percent of women in the United States can't reach orgasm during intercourse. Part of this has to do with the messages about sexuality they received growing up. Most mothers tell their daughters what *not* to do with their sexuality instead of how to enjoy it. Fortunately, the ability to have an orgasm can be learned.

The bottom line for men is this: a woman's orgasm is her choice. If she's incapable, that's not your fault. If she's holding back because of a relationship issue, she will usually make it known. If she tells you that it's her, and not you, she's probably telling the truth. You can't make anyone have an orgasm; you can only provide her with the kind of pleasuring she says she wants. In fact, if she senses that you're depending on her to have an orgasm, she may feel so pressured she won't be able to relax enough to have one. And if she fakes it, it usually means that she wants you to know that you do satisfy her.

It would be far better for the two of you to leave your expectations outside the bedroom door. If that feels too lonely, invite the spirit of adventure in for a little threesome, and let it loosen you up enough to let the sexual energy of the moment take you to places you've never been.

Faulty Idea 3: It's my partner's job to give me an orgasm, or "He's supposed to know about sex; I'm a 'good girl.'"

Everyone is responsible for his or her own orgasms. Period. If lack of learning is the problem, the graduated series of exercises in this book can help. If lack of orgasm signifies a relationship issue, marital counseling can get to the root of it. If you suspect a sexual problem may be biological, speak to your physician. Many prescription medications have sexually inhibiting effects. If you are a woman experiencing an overall lack of desire and you are taking birth control pills, talk with your physician; decrease in libido is a common side effect. Or, if you are not on the pill, consider meeting with a reproductive endocrinologist, who is knowledgeable about hormone disorders and how to treat them.

Faulty Idea 4: If she (he) doesn't have an orgasm (erection), she (he) doesn't love me, or "I'm not a valuable, worthwhile person if no one affirms me; I am unable or unwilling to affirm myself."

You are a couple, but you are also two separate people with individual needs and desires. Needing to have your partner perform in a certain way or to want exactly the same things you want means that your sense of self is on shaky ground. This will no doubt cause problems in other areas of your relationship, too.

Everyone feels insecure on occasion. We all need loving affirmation from our partners. But when you aren't making the effort to build your own self-esteem, your neediness can become so great it overwhelms your partner. The sad truth is that if you demand from your partner what you won't give to yourself, you will eventually push that person away. If you are honest with your beloved and allow yourself to be vulnerable enough to admit to your fears or insecurities, you will draw much closer together and you will feel the love and support you crave.

There is a world of difference between demanding (or manipulating) someone into giving you something you want and asking for it from a place of genuine honesty and vulnerability. This allows the other to empathize, let down his or her guard, and meet you tenderly instead of with resentment. It is only by revealing your real self—with doubts and fears—that intimacy grows deeper.

One good way to begin building self-esteem is to read John Pollard's book, *Self-Parenting: The Complete Guide to Your Inner Conversations.* We recommend it enthusiastically to our clients. It will help you replace any negative messages you give yourself with positive, self-affirming ones.

The exercises in the chapters ahead will add to your feelings of competence and self-worth and provide you with many opportunities to enjoy being physically close and feeling loved. For men especially, it is often easier to open up emotionally and mentally when you feel sexually embraced.

Self-loving exploration of the mindset you bring to bed, along with daily repetition of PC muscle exercises and overall good self-care, will lay the foundation for no-holds-barred pleasure. Then, to get from the foundation of erotic sensibility to the heights of sexual pleasure, just feel your way through the skill-building chapters ahead!

Self-Affirmation

Feeling good about yourself makes you irresistible to others. It's a real gift to enjoy the love of someone who loves you for you, and not for what you can give to him or her. However, it is hard to give that kind of love unless you are unconditionally accepting of yourself. And, frankly, few of us learned how to be that way in childhood. Most of us got mixed messages; now that we're grown up, we continue to browbeat ourselves.

Well, as one of our favorite bumper stickers says, it's never too late to have a good childhood. John Pollard's book, *Self-Parenting: The Complete Guide to Your Inner Conversations*, which we mentioned earlier, can be a great help here. To see whether you can benefit from Pollard's techniques, stop for a minute and pay attention to the things you say to yourself. Are they critical or positive? If they are self-negating, you can change them. Let's say that you catch yourself saying something to your partner that makes you cringe once it's out of your mouth. You could say, "Boy, are you stupid! What a dumb thing to say. He (or she) is going to think you're (stupid) (insensitive) (hateful)." Instead, it's much healthier to forgive yourself for making a mistake and to tell yourself, "I'll know better next time. It's okay to make a mistake. I'm still a good person."

Pollard's book goes into this in depth. For now, here are some affirmations to try repeating to yourself now and again.

"I am an honorable person. I do my best to be honest and genuine in life."

"I do my best at whatever task I try. If I don't succeed, I can keep working on it until I'm satisfied."

"I am unique in this world. I live my life in peace and let others do the same."

Chapter 5
Pleasure-Enhancing Control: A Program for Men

> It's not the men in my life that count—it's the life in my men.
>
> —Mae West, in *I'm No Angel*

How do you become so sexually synchronized as a couple that simultaneous orgasm is within your grasp whenever you want it? It starts with both of you becoming intimately aware of the nuances within your own sexuality and nudging your current limits to the outer edge of your potential. It also requires that the two of you work together, patiently and lovingly over time, to help each other map these nuances together.

The graduated series of exercises for men in this chapter and the corresponding exercises for women in Chapter 6 are designed expressly for this purpose. By setting aside time and making the commitment to do the solo and partner exercises, you will both develop the prowess to reach orgasm together whenever you want and deepen your pleasure in any physically intimate encounter. If sexual confidence has ever been a problem for you, you will find that issue vanishes as you work through this program. You may even find yourself in awe of the powerful, natural orgasmic force and your own ability to master it.

Men, this chapter is written specifically to you. I encourage you to also read your partner's chapter. If you both work on the solo exercises around the same time, you will both be prepared for (and excited about!) the mutual exercises that come later.

Before beginning each exercise session, refresh your senses with one of the relaxation techniques explained in the Chapter 4. If either of you feels tense prior to the exercise, do a sensate focus back caress (described in Chapter 3, page 54).

The Proven Program That Will Boost Your Staying Power

All right, guys, here are the goods! The program outlined in these pages will do more to boost your staying power and sexual confidence than any other I know. Best yet, each phase of this program will expand your capacity for pleasure. Anita and I are no fans of the coitus-interruptus, numbing-cream, think-of-something-distracting, testicle-tug schools of ejaculation control. We believe pleasure is what it's all about. When you have concluded this program, you should be able to last as long as you want, no matter what your partner does to you or how wildly out of control she becomes. You will also find that climaxing together, at will, becomes a natural extension of the closeness you will develop as you work through these exercises. Best yet, if you are highly motivated and schedule several sessions a week, you'll feel fabulous results in as little as six weeks.

There's just one catch: You really have to do these exercises, and in the order they are given. I know life is hectic, and there will be a temptation to skip them. Squelch this urge. You will have plenty of other, more wonderful temptations to pursue if you persist. Take the attitude that you are in training, like an athlete. Your goal? To reach the upper limits of your sexual capacity. Unlike other sports, this training will make you feel good every step of the way. We developed these exercises in our clinic because we were well aware of the ineffectiveness and unpleasantness of other techniques.

You may find certain aspects of the exercises repetitive. This is good. Through repetition you teach your body to make a habit of ejaculatory control.

How You Compare

Just mentioning premature ejaculation raises a lot of fear—and two questions: "Just how long do most men last anyway?" and "Am I normal?"

The best I can tell—from the numerous surveys we have reviewed—is that most men tend to last about seven minutes in intercourse, on average. This is fine, because if a woman is going to reach orgasm during intercourse, she'll typically do so within seven minutes. (Be aware that a great many women cannot reach orgasm during intercourse, so don't assume that you could have taken her there if you had lasted longer.) In light of those numbers, Masters and Johnson's definition that "A man has premature ejaculation if his partner fails to reach orgasm more than 50 percent of the time" is ludicrous.

Though it may not seem very long, seven minutes shows progress for the human male. When the Kinsey people studied staying power fifty years ago, their findings indicated that the average man lasted about three minutes in intercourse before ejaculating. Why only three minutes? The evolutionary remnants of natural selection could be the reason. Rapid ejaculation could once have conferred an evolutionary advantage: the more time early man spent in one spot, with his flanks exposed, the more likely he would get a bite taken out of him by an animal or human predator. Evolution aside, rapid ejaculation is culturally ingrained in us. Most boys feel a pressure to bring themselves off quickly when masturbating so they don't get caught.

Fortunately, habits can be changed. If a man's ability to experience sustained sexual pleasure were to be expressed in terms of a bell curve, the three-minutes-to-ejaculation outcome would be on the very bottom of the curve, leaving room for a lot more range than that. Men who have really mastered control can last for an hour or more during intercourse. That may not be as desirable as it sounds, however. Not all women like prolonged intercourse. The only way to know what your sweetheart likes is to ask her. (Having her show you is even better!)

Here are other sundry facts you might find helpful, if not downright comforting:

> On the average, younger men tend to ejaculate more quickly than older men. Ejaculatory response slows with age, which means you are likely to have more ejaculatory control at age thirty-five or forty than as a teenager or twenty-something.
>
> The level of sexual activity can affect ejaculatory control. If your libido outpaces your opportunity, rapid ejaculation is common.
>
> If you have a high sex drive, it is normal to ejaculate more quickly than usual the first time you are with a new partner.
>
> It is normal to ejaculate more quickly with intercourse than with manual stimulation or oral sex.

As you go along with the exercises that follow, become aware of what (either physically or mentally, alone or with your partner) finally pushes you over the edge into a climax. You may need these as *triggers* to help you climax at the moment when you desire an orgasm simultaneously with your partner. You should know your own triggers because once you have maximum ejaculation control and are lasting for a prolonged time, your penis will become somewhat desensitized and the psychological urgency to ejaculate will lessen. Triggers can be of use if you find yourself in the unusual situation of wanting to make yourself come rather than delay it. (The concept and use of triggers is discussed more fully in chapter 8.)

Ready, Set . . . Breathe

Effective, pleasure-enhancing ejaculation control requires three essentials. Keeping yourself relaxed is one of them. Becoming intimately aware of just how aroused you are is another. Knowing how to use your PC muscle is the third. If you are already doing the pelvic and PC muscle exercises every day, as explained in Chapter 4, you are off to a good start. If not, begin there first.

As you do those basic exercises, remember not to hold your breath or keep your muscles tense. If this is a problem for you, practice deep breathing before each exercise and whenever you think of it. Without relaxation and breath control, you will find it difficult to build staying power and won't receive the full benefit of the exercises. In the more advanced exercises you will actually use breath control as a technique to slow down or speed up your arousal.

The sensate focus touching technique outlined in this book helps promote relaxation and arousal awareness by focusing your mind on your sensations. That's why we use a sensate focus–style genital caress as the foundation for the exercises to come. You will need to set aside twenty minutes of private time for this caress.

♀ Exercise ♂
Basic Genital Caress

The purpose of this exercise is to discover your tactile senses and their receptivity for sensual pleasure. Think of this caress not as masturbation but as a new way of touching yourself.

Before You Begin Choose a time and place where you can be undisturbed for twenty minutes. If you are married and have children, ask your wife to ensure your privacy. If you are alone, turn off the phone, stereo, and anything that could disturb you. Make sure the room is warm and comfortable, and have on hand a good-feeling lubricant, such as massage oil or baby oil.

Begin by lying in bed or sitting comfortably in a chair. If you need to jump-start your arousal, it's fine to flip through an erotic magazine or watch an erotic video. Be patient with yourself. Since this is new, it might feel a bit awkward getting started.

The Exercise

1. Start with several belly breaths: Place one hand flat on your chest and the other on your abdomen. Breathe deeply so that the in-breath and out-breath each take several seconds. Make inhaling and exhaling one continuous process.

2. Take the lubricant, warm it in your palm, and slowly, sensually, stroke your inner thighs, scrotum, and all parts of your penis, including the head and the shaft. Don't use a hard, fast masturbation stroke or concentrate on stroking a particular area.

3. As you stroke, focus on the sensations you feel in each area that you touch.

4. Focus on how your hand feels as it does the touching.

5. Don't let anything distract you. If your mind begins to think about something else, bring it back to the point of contact between your hand and your body. It doesn't matter if you get distracted fifty times; each time, bring yourself back to the area you are touching. Keep your thoughts in the here and now—don't think about past or future.

6. As you caress yourself, keep your muscles, especially your PC muscle, as relaxed as possible. Feel how this relaxation adds to your pleasure and gives you a sense of control. Feel the calm power of energy that flows through relaxed muscles.

7. If twenty minutes feels like a long time and you get bored, try cutting the speed of your touch in half. Pay attention to the temperatures of your skin, the textures, the slope of your thighs, the curve of your penis.

8. If you feel aroused, breathe deeply and enjoy the sensations. It doesn't matter whether or not you get an erection or reach the point of inevitability. If you feel like ejaculating at the end of the session, go ahead. If not, take a few deep breaths and rest for a minute.

After the Exercise Ask yourself, "How much of the time was I able to focus and how much of the time was I thinking about something else?" Repeat this exercise every two to three days until you can relax and focus at least 50 percent of the time. Then move on to the exercise, Tuning in to Your Arousal, in the next section.

Developing Arousal Awareness

You're probably thinking, "Wait a minute. I know when I am aroused. What do I need an exercise for?" To an extent, you're right. But is your awareness surface knowledge or an accurate, precise appraisal? Can you focus in at any given moment and tell exactly how close you are to the grand climax? Can you soar and swoop among the heights of arousal like a magnificent eagle riding the currents of air? The degree of awareness I'm talking about is so finely honed, you can bank on it. The greater your precision, the greater your possibilities for control. (Practice comes into play here, too.)

When talking about arousal, one of the very first things you need to realize is that you can't equate how hard you are with how aroused you are. You can have a terrific erection but not be anywhere close to the point of inevitability. On the other hand, you can have a very soft erection and feel excited to the point of powerful orgasms. Erection is a measure of blood flow into the penis; arousal is your state of sexual excitement. They don't always correlate.

Let's concentrate on arousal level alone, first. The best way I know to differentiate your level is to liken your arousal continuum to some sort of scale. You can envision it, say, as a thermometer with the mercury rising as it heats up until it reaches the top. Whatever your analogy, give your scale levels from 1 to 10. A 1 equals no arousal, and a 10 is ejaculation and orgasm. A 2 or 3 refers to the twinges of arousal that take place as blood starts to flow into the penis. A 4 indicates a steady, low level of arousal. A 5 or 6 is medium arousal. By the time you reach 7 or 8, you probably feel your heart pound and your face flush, and you may be a little short of breath or beginning to sweat. A 9 is the point right before ejaculation, and a 10 is the magnificent explosion.

As you begin to develop arousal awareness, 1 and 10 won't be difficult to identify, but you may be less clear about the points in between. With practice, you will get better at recognizing and appreciating the shades of arousal, and you can enjoy the anticipation and erotic buildup at will.

♀ Exercise ♂
Tuning in to Your Arousal

Before you begin, secure your private space and time. Do some deep breathing to relax yourself.

1. Begin with the basic genital caress, just as before. Remember to take long, deep, slow breaths as you become aroused.

2. After a few minutes of caressing, stop and gauge your arousal level according to the arousal scale. Is it a level 2, a 5, a 3?

3. Resume your caress and stop again after a few more minutes. Is your arousal level higher, lower, or the same as before?

4. Continue caressing, stopping, and gauging your arousal for another fifteen minutes or so.

5. Notice how all your senses feel focused, tuned to yourself and your sexuality. Do you feel relaxed, energized, potent, and powerful?

6. If you'd like, finish the exercise with an orgasm, but don't think you have to. The point of the exercise is to begin developing arousal awareness, not arousing yourself to orgasm. Orgasm is simply a choice, as it will be in each subsequent exercise.

After you've done the Tuning in to Your Arousal exercise once, try the following manual "squeeze" version.

♀ Exercise ♂
The Arousal Awareness "Squeeze"

Set aside thirty minutes and secure your private space. Do some deep breathing to relax yourself.

1. Begin with the basic genital caress. Remember to take long, deep breaths.

2. After a few minutes of focusing on sensations, stop when your arousal climbs to level 7, or after ten minutes.

3. This time, when you stop to gauge your level of arousal, gently squeeze the head of your penis, just under the ridge that divides the head from the shaft, using your thumb and two fingers.

4. Continue caressing, stopping, gauging your arousal, and squeezing for another fifteen minutes or so.

Repeat this exercise every few days, with and without the manual "squeeze," until you are able to do the caress for fifteen to twenty minutes and recognize all your arousal levels between 1 and 10. This may take you two or three different sessions. When you feel comfortable with this exercise, you are ready to move on to the next step: peaking.

Peaking: Scaling the Heights, Teasing Back Down

The best way I know to rapidly gain control of ejaculation is to practice reaching certain heights of arousal then consciously bringing your arousal back down. It is a bit like riding a roller coaster, only in this case you are both the rider and the person at the controls. In sex therapy parlance, we call this practice "peaking." Instead of going straight to the top and falling over the edge, peaking lets you stretch out the time between initial arousal and ejaculation, so you experience several thrills of building arousal. Peaking stores up sexual charge and leads to deeper, more intense orgasms.

Pleasure-Enhancing Control

Later in this program, you will learn how to extend these pleasure peaks into longer plateaus, so you can draw them out until you have had your fill of anticipation and are ready for full-body release.

♀ Exercise ♂
Learning to Peak

Set aside thirty minutes and secure your private space. If you aren't relaxed, do some deep breathing.

1. Begin with a basic genital caress. (If you find that massage oil or other lubricants don't suit you, or if you want to experiment with something different, try using the inside of a banana peel. Don't laugh, I'm serious. Clients who have tried this love it. The creamy inside feels amazingly like a vagina. What you do is use the peel like a sheath, gripping it around your penis. Try playing around a bit and see what works for you.)

2. Slowly stroke your genitals, using sensate focus touch. Pay close attention to your sensations, without letting your fantasies or concerns keep you in your head.

3. When you reach arousal level 3, stop stroking and let your arousal slip back to level 1.

4. Begin stroking again and continue until you reach level 4 or 5. Then stop, take a deep breath, and let your arousal drop two levels, back to level 3.

5. To help bring your arousal level down between peaks, you can also help move the blood away from your genitals by slowing stroking your thighs in the direction away from your genitals.

6. Continue the exercise, taking yourself to higher and higher peaks each time. You may only be able to reach the lower levels the first few times you do this exercise, but try to reach levels 6, 7, 8, or even 9, if you can.

7. Each peak should take three to five minutes, so you should be able to fit in four to six peaks in a fifteen- to twenty-minute caress. Just remember to stay focused and to caress as slowly and sensually as you can. Don't forget to take a deep breath as you reach each peak.

Repeat this exercise every day or two until you are able to peak at levels 8 or 9.

Letting Your Lover Help

After you have practiced peaking on your own and feel confident in your arousal abilities, raise the stakes a bit. Ask your lover to join you in a practice session. Developing arousal awareness together puts you in sync with each other and that much closer to simultaneous orgasm. Working together is important for both of you, since your partner is just as likely to need practice in modulating her arousal, too.

Before you jump into the fun of practicing together, review the sensate focus principles (in Chapter 3, pages 52–54). Then talk about what each of you wants to accomplish from each session. Make a promise to remind each other at the beginning of each session that your goals are to play, have fun, and increase your pleasure together. Keep a sense of erotic joy with you as you do the exercises, and keep things light. Laugh together when things don't go quite the way you intend. Be patient with yourselves and each other.

There are several ways to approach partner exercises. If your lover is working through the next chapter and is ready to begin her partner exercises, make dates in which you try an exercise for each of you over the course of an hour or two. Try your exercise first, and make equal time for hers soon after. It works best to do yours first, so you can observe your arousal level from ground zero.

If your partner is not working through this program or is not ready for her partner exercises, begin each session by pleasuring her with sensate focus body caresses. If premature ejaculation is a chronic issue for you, sharing these caresses first will take away feelings of performance pressure.

♀ Exercise ♂
Basic Arousal Awareness à Deux

After securing your private time, breathe deeply together or slowly undress each other.

1. Give your partner a sensate focus caress to relax her. Keep it nongenital. Touch her slowly and lightly, concentrating on the smooth texture of her skin and the curves of her body. Spend twenty minutes or so with this.

2. Switch roles and have your partner caress you. Lie on your stomach while she caresses your back. She should caress slowly and for her own pleasure. If she's doing something you don't like, let her know; otherwise, just relax and enjoy being touched.

3. Notice whether you tense any muscles if you start becoming aroused, and have your partner tell you if she notices any tension. Consciously try to let go and relax as deeply as possible.

4. After about ten minutes, roll over onto your back and let your partner begin a front caress, slowly working her way down your body to your genitals.

5. As she strokes and caresses you, have her stop every few minutes and ask, "How aroused are you?" Tune in to yourself, tell her your arousal level, then let her begin caressing again.

6. Continue in this way for about fifteen minutes. Remember to keep your PC muscle relaxed throughout.

7. At the end of fifteen to twenty minutes, you can ask your partner to help bring you over the edge, if you'd like. If not, curl up with her and breathe deeply together for a few minutes. Maintaining warm contact as you come down grounds you together.

As you do this exercise, keep in mind that although you are with your partner, there is no need to show off or reach any certain arousal level. Be as free with her as you were with yourself. The whole point of sensate focus is to help you develop relaxed awareness.

Your partner can stroke you with her fingers and palms or use her mouth, if you're able to accept that much stimulation without needing release. In fact, if she is comfortable with oral sex, repeat this exercise until you can handle at least fifteen minutes of passionate oral play before it drives you over the edge. If you remember to focus on your sensations, breathe deeply when you feel aroused, and keep all your muscles relaxed, then lasting will be much easier. Then again, you might have more incentive not to!

♀ Exercise ♂
Start and Stop: Peaking with a Partner

Do whatever it takes to make sure you have at least an hour of uninterrupted time together. Take care to set an amorous mood you like. For some couples, this means candles and incense; for others, it means going out for a run together, returning sweaty and glowing.

Decide who goes first. If it's ladies first, let your partner explain what she wants during her half-hour. When it's your turn, explain that you want to play a game called Red Light, Green Light: She gets to do whatever she likes to arouse you (provided it is not uncomfortable), but the minute you tell her to stop, she must—and she can't start again until you tell her to.

1. Have your partner begin with a back caress, then turn over and let her stroke your chest, arms, and belly. Or, she could use her mouth and plant light, rapid lip and tongue flicks (or "butterfly kisses") wherever it pleases her. Let her be creative, while you focus on what you feel. Notice particularly what you feel in your penis, wherever her touch is.

2. When you reach arousal level 3, tell her "Red light." Then take a deep breath. Let your arousal slip down two levels before you say "Green light" and she starts again.

3. This time, allow yourself to reach level 5. Have your partner stop again, and wait until your arousal is down by two levels.

4. Continue in this way, peaking at levels 6, then 7, 8, and 9. Each peak, with its up and down phase, should take three to five minutes. Have your partner caress you slowly enough so that the peaks take this long. She can adjust her speed so that one peak takes a short time, the next peak takes longer, and so on.

5. After fifteen to twenty minutes of this, you may want to ejaculate. If you do, concentrate on the sensations and how they have deepened since you began these exercises.

Repeat this exercise in further sessions until you are able to go all the way through the arousal response cycle, from level 1 to 9, in a twenty-minute period.

• • •

Was that a welcome break from solo practice? Take a few minutes to reflect on what happened when you were with your partner the first time. Was it harder for you to stay focused on your arousal? Did it take longer to bring your arousal back down? Was it harder for your arousal to get started? Don't judge, just notice. Is there something you'd like to try differently next time?

The Power of PC (and I Don't Mean "Politically Correct"!)

The next part of this program requires you to return to solo practice for a while. Later, when you have become skilled at this, you will invite your partner in for another practice session. Be sure to take care with these next four exercises. They will teach you the fine art of using the PC muscle, a little muscle with huge importance.

The PC is the muscle that spasms when you ejaculate. When your body receives a certain level of stimulation, a reflex is triggered in the PC muscle. It spasms and causes semen to be ejected from the penis. At that point, the PC muscle response is involuntary. However, if you voluntarily squeeze the PC muscle when you reach certain levels of arousal, it acts like the brakes on a car and slows arousal down. You do have to squeeze the muscle in a particular way, and at the right time, or it won't work.

The following exercises will help you become skilled at the PC squeeze, so you can use it preemptively, even during passionate intercourse, to stop the spasm that leads to ejaculation and to prolong pleasure.

What's the best way to squeeze the muscle? There are three basic ways, and each man should try them all to find what works best for him. One approach is a long, hard squeeze held for several seconds. Another, which seems to work for most men, is two or three medium squeezes. The third approach is several quick, light squeezes in a row.

There are a few other things about the PC muscle you should know. The first time you use the squeeze, it may trigger an ejaculation. If this happens, don't worry about it; it won't happen again. Just wait a while, start the exercise over, and everything will be fine. Squeezing the PC muscle can also affect your erection: the PC muscle has to be relaxed for blood to flow into the penis and make it hard. If you continue to squeeze your PC as you are getting an erection, your erection will go down. As you do the following exercises, use your erection as a guideline for how best to squeeze your PC muscle. If you peak and then do a squeeze, try to squeeze just hard enough to take your arousal down without affecting your erection. With practice this will become much easier than it sounds.

♀ Exercise ♂
Peaking with the PC Muscle by Yourself

In this exercise, you will try various ways of using a PC muscle squeeze to see how they affect your arousal and increase your lasting power.

Take a few minutes to relax, clear your head, and get into your best sensate focus frame of mind. You will be starting with your old friend the genital caress, so use a lubricant that stays warm and feels good.

1. Begin a genital caress. Slowly stroke your penis and genital area, paying close attention to the sensations you feel.

2. When you reach arousal level 4, stop stroking, take a deep breath, and give your PC muscle one or two medium squeezes, exactly like you do when you exercise it every day.

3. The PC squeeze should help your arousal level go down. Let your arousal level dip back down to level 2.

4. Start the caress again and let your arousal level climb to level 5. This time, when you stop stimulation, take a deep breath and give your PC several quick, staccato-like squeezes.

5. Let your arousal level drop down to level 3.

6. Resume stroking again, and this time, rise to level 6 or 7. When you get there, stop stimulation, take a deep breath, and give one really hard squeeze. Hold it for about five seconds.

7. Continue the stroking-stopping-squeezing cycle as you peak at levels 7, 8, and 9.

In future sessions, you can repeat some of the levels if you want to and try the different types of squeeze at each level. This should help you figure out which squeeze method works for you. Ask yourself, "Which is most comfortable? Which is easiest to do? Which feels most natural? Which helps my arousal go down the fastest without affecting my erection?"

When you figure out your preferred PC squeeze method, work to perfect it!

The next three exercises offer important variations on using the PC muscle, and each will help you refine your control.

♀ Exercise ♂
Peaking with the PC Muscle Your Way

Before you begin, secure your private space and time. Do some deep breathing to relax and focus yourself.

1. Begin a genital caress. Do one of the previous peaking exercises by yourself for about twenty minutes.

2. Peak at arousal levels 4, 5, 6, 7, 8, and 9 as before, but this time, at each peak, use your preferred method. If you are, say, a medium squeeze type, when you reach each peak, stop stimulation, take a deep breath, and do two or three medium squeezes.

3. At each peak, allow your arousal to drop a couple of levels before resuming your strokes.

4. As your arousal builds, keep reaching for higher and higher peaks, until you reach the hot intensity of level 9.

♀ Exercise ♂
Climbing Higher and Higher with Your PC "Brake"

This exercise is much the same as the last, with one difference: You skip some of the lower levels so you can repeat peaks at those great higher levels. For instance, you may peak at arousal level 4, then 6, then 8, and then float between 8 and 9.

Before you begin, secure your private space and time. Do some deep breathing to relax and focus yourself.

1. Begin a genital caress. Do one of the previous peaking exercises by yourself for about twenty minutes.

2. Repeat several peaks at level 8, again using your PC muscle squeeze to drop your arousal.

3. Let yourself reach level 9, then try another squeeze.

4. If you ejaculate instead of slowing your arousal down, that's okay—control at level 9 will come with practice of this exercise.

Keeping It Up While You're Slowing It Down With this variation, you will gain more control. Until now, in each exercise you have stopped all stimulation at each peak, so your arousal would not go higher. In this exercise, as you reach each peak, you will continue to arouse yourself but you will use the PC squeeze to control your arousal level. This will help you reach a mastery with which you have control no matter what your partner does.

Before you begin, secure your private space and time. Do some deep breathing to relax and focus yourself.

1. Begin with a basic genital caress.

2. When you reach arousal level 4, continue to stroke yourself, take a deep breath, and squeeze your PC in the way that works best for you. Notice that squeezing your PC muscle will make your arousal level stay the same or go down a level.

3. Slow your caress down and let your arousal dip to level 2.

4. Speed the caress up a little, and this time, peak at level 6.

5. When you reach level 6, continue caressing yourself, take a deep breath, and squeeze your PC muscle. Notice that even though you continue to stimulate yourself, squeezing your PC muscle keeps your arousal level from climbing up.

6. Continue this exercise, doing similar peaks at levels 7, 8, and 9, if you can. If not, do several peaks at level 7 or 8.

Trying the PC Squeeze with Your Main Squeeze

When you have the PC squeeze technique down to your satisfaction, invite your partner back for a few more sexy practice sessions. Again, plan sessions of an hour or more, so that you each have half an hour to devote to your own exercises.

♀ Exercise ♂
Peaking with a Partner: Part Two

When it is your turn to work on an exercise, ask your partner if she's ready to play Red Light, Green Light, part two. As before, she will take the active touching or tonguing role and, as your arousal climbs the ladder, you will tell her each level. When you speak, she is to stop caressing you—and not start again until you give the word.

1. Lie on your back and consciously relax all of your muscles.

2. Have your partner begin a sensate focus caress of your chest that works its way down to your genitals. She can be creative—stroking you with her hands, her fingertips, her hair, her lips, or her tongue.

3. When your arousal reaches level 4, tell your partner. That's her cue to stop.

4. Take a deep breath, squeeze your PC muscle, and notice as your arousal level falls.

5. When your arousal hits level 2, let her start the caress again. This time, let your arousal reach level 5 or 6 before you tell your partner.

6. When she stops, take a deep breath and squeeze your PC muscle. Again, when your arousal drops two levels, have her begin stroking again.

7. Continue this stroking-peaking-squeezing cycle at levels 7, 8, and 9 for another twenty minutes or so.

♀ Exercise ♂
Partner Peaking: An Advanced Variation

This is a more advanced version of the peaking exercise you did by yourself, in which you continued stimulation after doing a PC muscle squeeze. In this exercise, you enjoy stimulation from your partner. Mastering this exercise is a milestone along the path to total control.

1. Begin the exercise above, Peaking with a Partner: Part Two, but tell your partner that this time she doesn't have to stop her tantalizing touch.

2. At each peak, take a deep breath, squeeze your PC, and notice how hard and how long you have to squeeze to send your arousal down or stay at the same level while your partner continues caressing you.

3. Practice several peaks every few minutes at levels 4, 5, 6, 7, 8, and 9.

It may take a few sessions with this exercise until you can peak at all levels and control your arousal using the PC muscle. That's perfectly normal. You will find there are much less desirable ways to spend an evening with your lover!

Plateauing: Making Pleasure Peaks Last Longer

The term "plateauing" may sound flat, but you will certainly like what it means. Plateauing exercises help you stretch out pleasurable peaks so they last anywhere from a few seconds to several minutes. There are several techniques you can use to turn your peaks into longer plateaus: changing your breathing, using your PC muscle, changing your movement, and changing your focus. I suggest you practice only one of these techniques at a time until you really get the hang of it. When you've got one, move on to the next. When you've mastered them all, try doing several plateaus combining the techniques. As with your first peaking exercises, you will begin by yourself, then move to perfecting the pleasure with your partner.

♀ Exercise ♂
Plateauing by Yourself: Breathing

Before you begin, relax, breathe deeply, and focus your thoughts.

1. Begin with a genital caress, and do a simple peak at arousal level 4.

2. When you reach level 4, stop stimulation, take a deep breath, and allow your arousal to fall back to level 2.

3. Begin stroking again, and try to plateau at just beyond level 5 by changing your breathing. Don't stop your caress—instead, breathe

as slowly as you can for a few breaths. This should lower your arousal about half a level.

4. When you drop to just above level 4, start to breathe faster, almost as if you were panting. Feel how this raises your arousal.

5. Try to hover at level 5 for a few seconds.

6. When you want to increase your arousal, speed up your breathing. To prolong it, slow your breathing down.

Try to plateau for about twenty seconds, but don't do it any longer than that or you might hyperventilate.

Once you feel comfortable with breath control, try combining it with the PC muscle squeeze. Since you have practiced the squeeze a lot, it should come easily.

♀ Exercise ♂
Plateauing by Yourself: PC Squeeze

This exercise is the same as the previous one, but it introduces your basic arousal moderator, the PC squeeze.

1. Relax, focus, and begin a genital caress. Continue your caress until you reach a point just beyond level 6, then give your PC muscle a couple of light squeezes. This should cause your arousal level to drop about half a level.

2. When you drop to a point slightly below level 6, relax your PC muscle and continue your stroking.

3. When you reach level 6 again, use a PC squeeze to bring yourself down.

4. Alternate between squeezing and relaxing your PC, and see if you can hover at level 6 for thirty seconds to a minute.

♀ Exercise ♂
Plateauing by Yourself: Switching Strokes

This exercise takes a different approach to prolong pleasure: switching strokes.

1. Relax, focus, and begin a genital caress. Build your arousal until halfway past level 7, then slow down your strokes and let your arousal drop to just below 7.

2. Use a faster stroke to bring yourself back to level 7.

3. See if you can plateau at level 7 for thirty seconds to a minute just by changing the speed of your stroke. If you want to go to a higher level, stroke faster. To go lower, go slower.

♀ Exercise ♂
Plateauing by Yourself: Changing Your Focus

Now you are ready for the final plateauing technique: the subtle ability to touch one area and focus on another.

1. Relax, focus, and begin a genital caress, and plateau to arousal level 8. During your plateau, continue slowly stroking your penis, but as you do, shift your focus to an area that you are not touching. For instance, if you are stroking the head to get yourself to level 8, shift the focus of your attention to your testicles.

2. This shift in focus ought to cause your arousal level to drop half a level. When it does, bring your focus back to the area that you are touching.

3. See if you can plateau at level 8 for thirty seconds to a minute by changing your focus. If you want to become more aroused, focus on the point of contact. If you want to feel less aroused, shift your focus away from it.

All this isn't as easy as it sounds, is it? But later, with your lover, you will find it so satisfying. You're probably ready to stop at this point. Repeat these exercises, as you can, until you are able to do them automatically without having to really think about them. Practice combining the techniques until you can automatically incorporate two, three, or even all of them. For example, see if you can keep yourself at level 7 or 8 for thirty seconds or more by using a PC squeeze and slowing down both your stroke and your breathing.

Sensation Management Through Switch Focus

One of the most challenging techniques you can learn that simultaneously enhances ejaculatory control and overall pleasure is called switch focus. Switching focus is different from changing focus, but these techniques are sometimes confused even by professionals. (In fact, both these exercises are sometimes confused with the useless or destructive "Think of Something Non-Sexual" method tried by some men to retard ejaculation. That method can actually speed up the time of ejaculation and even condition a man to become aroused by undesirable stimuli.) The essence of changing focus is the shifting of attention from the area of immediate physical contact to one where no contact is occurring. Switching focus, as we explain below, lets you experience the point of actual contact in many different ways and combinations.

Many men experiencing premature ejaculation or erection difficulty tend to focus only on their genitals or impending ejaculation. This causes an even greater genital tension and, therefore, will actually speed up the ejaculation or reduce the erection response. Through switch focus, you practice gaining pleasure from many sources of stimulation, either at one time or in combinations.

Switching focus actually requires you to pay closer attention to your pleasure. The metaphor I always use is that of a symphony: you can listen to the overall sound produced by all the instruments at once, or you can listen very intently to the violin or the flute, or you can go back and forth between listening to individual instruments and the full sound of the whole orchestra. In this way, you appreciate all aspects of the music.

With sex, it is the same. You can focus on the overall warm feeling of your bare skin against your partner's, the flutter of her lips on yours, the slickness of how wet she is inside, the push you feel in the head of your penis when you thrust, or the sound of her voice as it registers your touch. When working on sensuous awareness exercises alone, you can switch your focus from the head of your penis to the shaft, to your testicles, to the skin on your thighs, or to the feeling in your hand as you pleasure yourself. Then practice putting these sensations together in combinations of two or more.

To develop this ability, try the switch focus technique with yourself first before attempting it with your partner.

Tips on the Switch Focus Technique

- Before doing anything, take time to relax and still your mind. Take a few deep breaths, or shrug your shoulders. You really need to put all other thoughts out of your mind to focus fully on the here and now of sexual sensations.

- In solo practice, try switching focus from what your hand feels like caressing your genitals to what your genitals feel like as they are caressed by your hand.

- When practicing with your partner, lie side-by-side and fondle each other. Practice switching focus from your hand to your partner's hand and from your genitals to your partner's genitals. This ability to switch focus will help you to last longer by increasing your ability to plateau at any level. It will also multiply the many pleasures you experience in sex and teach you to savor the differences among them.

Once the switch focus technique is established in your repertoire, you have all the techniques you need to keep yourself at any level of arousal you choose, whether you are pleasuring yourself or making love to your sweetheart. This means it's about time to schedule another practice session with her.

♀ Exercise ♂
Creating Plateaus with Your Partner

Begin this exercise by having your partner caress your back, chest, and belly. Then let her pleasure you in the way you like best.

1. As you begin to reach arousal level 5, get ready to change your breathing. When you reach a point slightly above level 5, slow down your breathing until your arousal level dips just below 5.

2. Speed up your breathing so that you are almost panting. This will cause your arousal level to rise slightly past 5.

3. Practice manipulating your breathing for about twenty seconds so that you hover around a level 5. If you want to lower your arousal, breathe slower. If you want to heighten it, breathe faster. Your partner should not change what she is doing, but should continue caressing with her hands or mouth in a way that both of you enjoy.

4. When your arousal climbs past level 6, squeeze your PC muscle.

5. As you dip down below level 6, relax your PC muscle and enjoy the stimulation.

6. When you climb higher than level 6, use the PC squeeze technique again. See if you can plateau at level 6 for thirty seconds or more using your PC muscle. If you want to go to a lower level, squeeze your PC muscle. If you want to go higher, relax your PC muscle.

7. Try the next plateau at level 7. This time, you will need your partner's cooperation. When your arousal rises past level 7, ask your partner to slow her stroking. Focus on her slower touch until your arousal dips below 7. Then tell her to go faster.

8. Once your arousal rises above level 7, see if you can plateau there for thirty seconds or more by telling your partner whether you'd like her to go faster or slower. It won't take much change in speed for you to plateau at any level for thirty seconds to a minute.

9. As a final peak, change your focus. Let your arousal rise just past level 8. When you feel it rise past level 8, switch your focus from the intensity of your genitals to an area that isn't being touched. For instance, switch your focus to what it feels like to have her leg rub against yours or her hair brush your shoulder.

10. See if you can plateau at level 8 by switching your focus back and forth between the area being caressed and other areas of your body. To drive your arousal level higher, focus on where your are being stroked. To diminish it, focus on a different area.

By the end of this exercise, you may feel highly energized or very spent—or both, because you get a real workout in this session. Repeat this exercise with your partner the next day or a few days later. Try to use a different plateauing technique at different levels, or combine techniques as you go.

Be creative, and have fun. You and your partner can create your own plateaus and challenge each other. See what combinations you can do and which ones you enjoy the most. In a third or fourth session, try to use all four plateauing techniques at the same time.

Maintaining Control during Intercourse: The Ultimate Test

If you have completed all the exercises to this point, congratulate yourself! Think back on how far you have come. What is possible for you now that was not before you began this program? What new sexual delights have you discovered?

The point of these exercises, of course, is to help you achieve the kind of control that is necessary for simultaneous orgasm. But you have one more challenge ahead of you—mastering the use of these techniques during regular intercourse and actually incorporating all that you have learned into your sex life. Certain intercourse positions, such as vaginal rear-entry and man-on-top, will make this more difficult, so begin with the more basic positions. They will give you a better opportunity to remember what you've learned, so that everything becomes second nature—even during the most intense, control-defiant sexual activities.

Ironically, the traditional man-on-top, or missionary, position challenges a man's control because it creates a lot of physical tension. Any man who is supporting his whole weight with just his elbows and knees is bound to be very tense, and tension, as I've said before, leads to rapid ejaculation. Being on top may also make you feel pressure to perform. We generally recommend that you attempt to lie flat on your partner and use pelvic rolls and thrusts as compared to the push-ups required when you support your weight on your arms. Again, whenever you're anxious to please, you lose ground in the ejaculation control department.

So, to start with, try the no-fail, side-to-side position.

♀ Exercise ♂
Side-to-Side Loving

While this is an easy position for retaining control, it may take a little doing to get the position just right. So you and your partner might want to get the position down before you start the exercise.

To get into position, lie on your side facing your partner. Your partner will lie on her back perpendicular to you, with one of her legs on top of yours and the other leg between yours. She should be comfortable, with her hips relatively flat on the bed. If she has to twist, switch legs.

Before You Begin Set aside an hour for the exercise. Begin by lying side-to-side. You can start by doing a back and front sensate focus style caress on your partner, if that's what she wants, or she may want help with a specific exercise of her own instead.

1. When it is your turn, have your partner caress your back for a few minutes. Then turn over. As she fondles you, enjoy your building arousal until you peak at level 4.

2. At that moment, have her stop stimulating you and let your arousal drop a couple of levels.

3. Have her start again, and peak at level 4 a couple more times. Let

yourself peak at level 5 or 6 before you get into position for intercourse. It doesn't matter whether you have a full erection or not. When you begin intercourse in the side-by-side position, you can insert your penis no matter how erect you are. Just be sure to use lubricant, so you don't hurt your partner.

4. When you are inside her, lie together without moving and breathe a few moments, so you can notice just how wonderful it feels to be joined like this. While you may be tempted to skip the sensate focus–style caress or the peaking part of this exercise, don't. If you do, the exercise loses its impact. Your body is learning to carry its new knowledge over to intercourse.

5. Let your arousal drop down to level 4, then start thrusting slowly. Remember to breathe, focus on what you are feeling, and keep all of your muscles (thigh and PC especially) relaxed. Your partner should follow your movements but not thrust on her own.

6. When you reach level 6, stop thrusting, take a deep breath, and relax all of your muscles. Allow your arousal to drop a couple of levels, back to level 4 or so. Stopping the stimulation should allow your arousal level to go down. If it doesn't, pull all the way out of your partner. Now see if you can repeat another peak at level 7. Slowly thrust until you are at level 7, then stop, breathe, and relax all your muscles. If you can peak at level 8 and 9 during this exercise, go on and do that, too.

7. After doing step 6 for a while, you may choose to finish with an ejaculation or simply stop. Either choice is equally satisfactory as far as the success of the exercise goes.

♀ Exercise ♂
Using the PC Muscle for Control

You have already practiced using the PC squeeze to control your arousal during foreplay. Using this technique during intercourse raises a new question, however: Should you squeeze on the in-stroke or the out-stroke?

This becomes a matter of individual style and preference, acquired through practice and experience. Some men like to squeeze on the in-stroke as they penetrate deepest into the vagina. (Your partner might feel this as a pleasurable flick.) Others prefer to squeeze on the out-stroke as they lie back and relax the rest of their muscles. You can also squeeze somewhere between the out-stroke and the in-stroke. Practice to see what works best for you. Using the PC squeeze during this exercise will allow you to thrust noticeably faster and harder than you did in the previous exercise.

1. Begin with senate focus–style caresses. Then have your partner pleasure you, until you peak at arousal level 5 or 6.

2. Do a couple of easy, relaxed peaks at level 5 or 6, using your PC muscle at each peak to take you down a level.

3. Get into a side-to-side position and insert your penis into your partner, using lots of lubricant.

4. This time, at each peak, stop stimulation and squeeze your PC muscle in the way that works best for you. With each peak, stop moving, breathe, squeeze, and relax all your muscles. Allow your arousal level to go down a level or two. Then start again and try to do a higher-level peak.

5. Continue peaking. See how many peaks you can do. See if you can peak at 7, 8, or 9 without stopping the stimulation and by using the PC muscle.

At the end of the exercise, you can let yourself ejaculate, if you like. Practice this exercise until you can do four or five peaks in this position.

Side-to-Side Intercourse with Continued Stimulation Remember when you worked solo and learned to peak by squeezing the PC muscle while you continued to stroke yourself? You can do the same thing during intercourse. Try it first, in the side-by-side position. This time, as you reach each peak, continue thrusting while squeezing your PC muscle in the way that works best for you. You will probably find that all of the peaks start to run together and you squeeze as needed while having continuous intercourse.

♀ Exercise ♂
The Trident Position

Are you ready for a new position? This is a different version of the man-on-top position than you may be used to. In the standard missionary position, your partner lies flat on her back and you lie on top of her. In this position, she lies on her back, puts her legs up in the air, bends her knees, and spreads her legs—while you kneel between her legs and get as close to her as you comfortably can and penetrate deeply into her vagina.

In this position, your center of gravity rests in your legs and hips. If you wish, you can brace yourself against your partner's legs with your arms, but you shouldn't need to support any of your weight with your chest and arms. This position leaves you free to enjoy all the sensations of intercourse and it gives you more freedom of movement. You are also able to withdraw easily if you need to. Try out the position with your partner before you begin the exercise, so you won't struggle with it later.

Before You Begin Make sure you are relaxed, grounded, and energized for deep pleasure.

1. Begin with sensate focus caresses or your partner's exercise, if she's working on her program.

2. Do a couple of easy, low-level peaks with whatever stimulation you feel like.

3. Get into the side-by side position and do a couple of medium-level peaks.

4. Change to the trident position and try a couple of peaks. If you can do two peaks in the new position, consider yourself a success.

5. The first time you use the trident position, just do basic peaks in which you reach a specific level, stop the stimulation, breathe, and relax all your muscles so your arousal drops one or two levels.

6. The next time you do the exercise, try to do all of your peaks using the PC muscle squeeze.

7. The third time, try doing all of your peaks using the PC muscles while continuing to thrust.

At this point, you can simply stop—the exercise is a great success—or you can continue to an ejaculation.

With each successive exercise, you will probably notice three things. First, it will take you longer to reach each peak. Second, you will need to squeeze your PC muscle less hard. Third, you will be able to thrust harder and faster. Soon, you will find yourself being aware of your arousal throughout continuous stimulation—thrusting without stopping or even slowing down. This is where the pleasure lies!

♀ Exercise ♂
Plateauing with Intercourse

The trident position is great to use to extend your intercourse arousal peaks into gratifying plateaus.

Before You Begin To help your body link the learning from the previous exercises to intercourse, you need to start with the sensate focus caresses and manual and oral pleasuring again.

1. Do a couple of preliminary peaks, as before.

2. Switch to the trident position.

3. Try to plateau around arousal level 6 or 7, using changes in your breathing. See if you can hover at level 6 or 7 just by changing your breathing.

4. Now try a plateau using your PC muscle. If you want to go lower, squeeze the PC muscle. If you want to go higher, relax the PC muscle and continue thrusting. See if you can hover in a very narrow arousal range by doing this.

When that is comfortable for you, experiment with changing your movement and switching your focus during intercourse. You are going to need to refine both techniques a bit. When you reach a new plateau, slow down your movement to give yourself control. To go higher, speed up your movement. This version of the man-on-top position is good to use because you have a full range of movement, so it's easy to slow down or speed up. To plateau by changing focus, shift your focus from the area of the penis that is most aroused to an area that is less aroused.

In any exercise, if you have peaked and plateaued for twenty to thirty minutes, go ahead and ejaculate if you feel like it. Don't pressure yourself if you don't feel like it.

• • •

As you get better at plateauing during intercourse, have your partner gradually increase her movement. You can also experiment with different positions that are a little more challenging. Here are some tips that will help:

> You will probably find that you can do this better in the traditional missionary position (your partner lies on her back and you lie on top of her). Make sure your full weight is on your partner and that you thrust using just your pelvis. (Remember the pelvic rolls you practiced from Chapter 4.)

> If your partner is on top, watch the tendency to arch your back off the bed and tense your leg muscles. Try instead to keep your buttocks and lower back flat on the bed and thrust using just your pelvis.

> Save the rear-entry position for when you are really feeling confident. This position is tricky because it is so psychologically stimulating, at least for most men. You can maintain control, however, if you pace yourself, keep your center of gravity in your legs and hips, and pull out whenever you need to.

In any new position, if you have difficulty maintaining the kind of control you want, just retrace all of your steps. The first time you do the position, try at first to stay inside without moving. Then try two simple peaks. The next time, peak with the PC muscle and move harder and faster. The time after, try to use the PC as you keep moving. Finally, try to plateau, adding in one plateauing technique at a time. Soon you will be able to achieve ejaculation control in any position, if you approach it systematically. Eventually, it won't feel so mechanical—you will simply delight in the variety now available to you.

Bringing it all Together

That's the program. If you are highly motivated to improve your staying power, this little in-home instruction course ought to do the trick. In fact, if you had good ejaculatory control at the start, you will be surprised at how much you are able to increase your pleasure and intensify your orgasms. If you didn't have great ejaculatory control at the beginning, you should be pleased with and proud of the gains you've made. (See the Appendix for a visual conception of this improvement.)

After working your way through this program, if premature ejaculation is still a problem, consider consulting a certified sex therapist or qualified psychotherapist to help resolve the underlying problem. Short-term, inexpensive therapy is available, and you shouldn't hesitate to seek it out. Just remember to be discerning. You and your partner owe it to yourselves to overcome the problem.

Expect a great payoff in your intimate relationship as well. Your efforts tell your partner you really care about her. Her willingness to be of help is a return compliment. Even better, if she has been learning how to peak and plateau along with you, you have the necessary prerequisites to learning how to reach orgasm together.

A Word to Women

Learning to improve ejaculatory control can be an anxiety-provoking process for your partner, so be supportive. Here are a few ways you can help.

Help him have the privacy and space to do his solo exercises. You will get the same consideration from him when it's time for your exercises. Make a pact with him to give him time, free from responsibilities, such as house chores or the kids' interruptions, so he can do his exercises alone.

Come to the partner exercises with a spirit of play and learning and without expectations. If he needs you to stop stimulating him or to disengage from intercourse to reduce his arousal level, please do as he asks. Remember, this is only a temporary phase, and it is leading to something much better. Concentrate on the pleasure of your own experience in each given moment. Realize, too, that you are also learning to modulate your arousal as you help him modulate his.

Because this is a graduated program, the exercises are in a specific order so that sexual learning can build in stages. Encourage your lover to do the exercises in sequence, as outlined, without skipping the details or cutting corners, to help optimize his body's ability to learn.

Finally, if you are not into "marathon" intercourse, tell him so straight out. It could be that he's making all of this effort simply to please you. Let him know exactly what pleases you and what doesn't so he can redirect his efforts if need be. Sexual pleasure is a two-way street, and to reach simultaneous orgasm you and your partner must embrace and own your sexual powers.

Chapter 6
Pleasure-Enhancing Release: A Program for Women

> The most holy thing you can do is live with pleasure. Enjoy your food, enjoy your sex. It's where the life force is.
>
> —Gioia Timpanelli, poet, at the Omega Institute, Rhinebeck, New York, June 8, 1985

If the idea of simultaneous orgasm sounds great to you but the reality seems remote—because you are not one of those fortunate women who pops like a cork during sex—don't worry. You are not alone. More than 50 percent of all sexually active women in the United States are unable to reach orgasm during intercourse. Even if you are in that group, you are not fated to remain there for life. You can learn how to be orgasmic during intercourse and, better yet, how to have multiple orgasms. You just need to give yourself time for your deep, feminine sexual nature to unfold, using the following exercises and guidelines, and you will never have to worry again about whether you are going to come or whether he will lose patience before you do.

This chapter can help you maximize your existing sexual pleasures, find some new ones, and enable the release of your orgasmic potential. It starts with a reawakening of your sexuality and desire. Next, you will learn some cognitive steps to greater sexual freedom. Finally, there are a number of solo and partner-oriented interactions that bring it all together.

If you are orgasmic already but wish to further explore the range of sexual pleasure available to you, the path is well-marked in the pages ahead. Together, we will look at ways you can achieve the following:

- Release past conditioning that may be interfering with the full expression of your sexuality

- Recover the unselfconscious sensuality of childhood

- Discover the kinds of touch, talk, and sex play that take you over the edge

- Bring yourself to climax, alone or with a partner, by stimulating one or more of your pleasure centers (we have some brand new techniques that really work!)

- Experience a relatively unknown, power-packed orgasm that really satisfies

In Chapter 7, we will uncover the secrets of multiple orgasm and, in Chapter 8, we will explain how to modulate your arousal so that you can climax at the precise moment you want to. If you believe you are already fully and satisfactorily orgasmic, you may wish to skim this chapter and proceed to Chapter 7. However, we strongly suggest that you read and do the exercises in the sections on Arousal Awareness, Peaking, and Plateauing.

Why Many Women Have Difficulty with Orgasm

Why is it that so many women have difficulty reaching orgasm at all, let alone during intercourse? Why is it that men find it so much easier to climax? There are several reasons. One has to do with evolution and the conservative nature of Nature. Men must climax if they are going to inseminate women and help perpetuate the species. It serves evolution to make this process automatic for men. But a woman can get pregnant without having an orgasm. In fact, some women never experience vaginal orgasm until they give birth. That's right: Birthing is an orgasmic experience, even through the pain. (Later in this chapter, the Female Ejaculatory Orgasms and Childbirth section further discusses this phenomenon.)

Another reason women may not reach orgasm during intercourse is that many reach orgasm through clitoral stimulation, and it isn't always easy to receive enough during intercourse. Some women seem to have more sensitivity in their vaginas and others in their clitoris and labia.

Nature and physiology aside, the main obstacle to female orgasm is lack of self-knowledge. This usually springs from outdated, puritanical, or misogynistic beliefs which are ignorant and fear-based attempts to curb the awesome power of female sexuality. These may be compounded by negative sexual experiences, such as sexual molestation, abuse, and rape.

Few of us grow up in homes where female sexuality is talked about. We talk about men going out and getting laid, and we talk about women growing up and getting married. How are women supposed to become orgasmic if they never touch their bodies to find out what pleasures them? Others of us do it in secret and with shame. When I was a little girl, I'd say, "God, I'll just do it this one last time. Don't banish me to hell." Then, of course, I'd masturbate again.

No matter what the source, damaging beliefs inhibit many women from allowing themselves to fully surrender to this ecstatic experience of orgasm, and yet, being orgasmic is a potential within every woman. If there is truth to that old Joni Mitchell song that "we are stardust, we are golden" and truth to the ancient Vedic texts that say whole universes reside within us, then isn't it only natural that women, too, are wired to experience cosmic explosions during the act that brings new life into being?

Orgasm 101: The Act in All Its Varieties

At the center of the potentially transformative and ecstatic orgasm is a whole mind-body sequence of events. First, sexual arousal builds, causing the erectile tissue in the clitoris and the inner and outer vaginal lips to swell with blood. The pressure of the blood vessels in the muscles surrounding the vaginal walls causes the body to release lubricating vaginal fluids. The middle section of the vagina may tighten while the inner third opens, to help accommodate the penis. The uterine muscles may tighten.

At the point of climactic release, the muscles surrounding the uterus and cervix contract involuntarily, making the abdomen flutter and pull in. The neck, arms, and legs may also spasm, as blood pressure, heart rate, and breathing reach their peak. At the same time, a feeling of warmth suffuses the genitals, spreading up through the heart and beyond. Orgasmic sensations can range from subtle to strong.

Psychologically, one can experience a feeling of release and perhaps fluidity or expansiveness. Some women report entering into states of altered or "unity" consciousness during particularly ecstatic moments.

Other women report having multiple orgasms, or orgasms that originate at different trigger points and provide pleasurable feedback from each. Also within the realm of female sexual experience are ejaculatory orgasms, which originate at the Grafenberg spot or G-spot (named for Dr. Ernst Grafenberg, who first made specific reference to it) in the vagina and can cause the release of a large amount of fluid. G-spot orgasms can be very intense and can cause a woman to feel so fully satisfied that she's ready to take a break from sex for a few minutes to several days or longer.

Individual women's trigger spots vary tremendously. They include the clitoris, the G-spot, the nipples, the labia, and even the mind, by itself. Gina Ogden, Ph.D., author of *Women Who Love Sex*, may have been the first to scientifically document that some women are capable of reaching orgasm just by "thinking off," as she calls it. As she writes in her book, her findings "challenge the most sacred tenet of sex research: the notion that sexual pleasure is centered in the genitals and depends on physical stimulation."[1]

The "Yes, I Can" Approach

If women can use their minds to "think off," unfortunately they can also use it to turn off. One of the biggest problems I've seen during my many years in clinical practice is the sexual clutter women carry around in their brains. Because of the beliefs we have inherited from a patriarchally-oriented society, our communities, and our families, which are filters for social beliefs, our sexual identity is often fragmented and distorted. It takes conscious work to repair this damage and reclaim our sexual identities.

To begin this process, I often use the following visualization exercise with my clients. Read the visualization into a tape recorder (or have a friend with a soothing voice read it for you) and then use it. Relax and play the tape during special sessions you set aside for yourself. Realize that these sessions are not just for you—as you resolve damaging attitudes and beliefs about female sexuality, you also open the way to greater sexual health for your daughters and sons and the women who come after you. (This exercise is similar to the Exploring Your Adolescent Sexuality exercise described in Chapter 3.)

♀ Exercise ♂
Reconnecting with Sexuality, Reawakening Desire: A Guided Imagery Exercise

Before You Begin Take a few moments to relax and get comfortable. Sit in a comfortable chair or lie down, loosen tight clothing and jewelry, and take the phone off the hook. If you are married, ask your husband to ensure your privacy. Take slow, deep belly breaths until you are conscious of the natural flow of your breath—inhaling, exhaling, inhaling, exhaling. You may be surprised at how easily breathing alone can produce a state of gentle relaxation.

When You Are Ready When your body "breathes itself" slowly, easily, deeply, according to its own natural rhythm, let your eyes close. Begin this exercise with a signal breath, a message that tells your body you are ready to enter a deep state of relaxation. To take a signal breath, breathe in sharply (through your nose if you can) and exhale fully through your mouth. You may notice a tingling sensation when you do this. This is your body's way of acknowledging the advent of deep relaxation.

The Visualization As you concentrate on your breathing, imagine a ball of pure energy or white light that forms in your lower abdomen. As you inhale, it rises up the front of your body to your forehead. As you exhale, it moves down your spine, down your legs, and into the ground. Again, imagine this ball of energy or light traveling up your body as you inhale and down your spine and legs, into the ground as you exhale.

Pleasure-Enhancing Release

Circulate this ball of energy around your body for a few minutes and let its circulation move you into a state of deeper relaxation and comfort. Each time you inhale and exhale you may be surprised to find yourself twice as relaxed as you were a moment before—twice as comfortable, twice as peaceful. With each breath, every fiber of your body eases. All the tightness, tension, pain, and discomfort drains down your spine, down your legs, and into the ground. Let this energy circulate around.

(Pause here for a few minutes to repeat the breathing cycle.)

As your body enjoys this nice state of deep relaxation, allow your mind to go to a place of peace and beauty. It can be your favorite place, indoors or out, or one you'd like to visit. It is peaceful, serene, secure: a special place. When you are there, let an image of your sexuality emerge, an image of your sexuality before society or parents told you anything was wrong or bad. This sexuality is an image of pure joy, a part of your inner child that is playful and noncritical. It is excited about doing things; it is looking forward to them; it has a positive attitude. Allow this pristine sexuality to surround you, and accept it. Be at peace with it.

Now form a symbol of your sexuality that you can draw when you open your eyes. Anytime you start feeling tense or worried after this session, you can look at the symbol and remember the part of you that is free, fun, and pure—there is no judgment. Place that free part where you can retrieve it, in your brain or in your heart.

Now that you have freed your sexuality, allow a feeling of desire to flow through your body, free from embarrassment, fear, or negative feelings. Let the unadulterated desire spread through your body. You may feel as if a soft pulsation or a warm mist is invigorating you.

As you did with the white light, let your desire circulate around your body, up your head and down to your back, and allow it to build in intensity, slowly, steadily, until you feel a ball of pleasure that explodes, enveloping your entire body. Let feelings of rejuvenation and fulfillment replace the desire, and be at peace.

If you would like, repeat this visualization and allow yourself to gently open to the intensity of it.

(Pause to allow time to repeat the cycle.)

Make a date with yourself to do this visualization again tomorrow. Now picture yourself back in that place that feels special and safe, and when you are ready, open your eyes and come back to the room. This would be a good time to draw the symbol you visualized and write down your feelings.

Ridding Yourself of Faulty Beliefs That Inhibit Your Sexuality

The image you generated in the visualization exercise above will give you a touchstone of your healthiest sexual self that you can return to whenever you need to. You may also need to work on any faulty, negative attitudes that clutter around this healthy sexual self-identity.

The way I see it, orgasm is an attitude. *You will only feel as much sexual pleasure as you allow yourself to have.* In fact, you can do the most advanced sex exercises on the planet, and do them until you are blue in the face, but if you hold beliefs that limit your sexual pleasure or freedom, you still may not reach orgasm when you desire. This next set of exercises will help you separate out your unique sexual identity from the beliefs you've inherited from others. Once you consciously evaluate and decide in your mind what your sexual attitudes and values are, and then reinforce them with affirmations, you won't have to continue to be influenced by faulty learning. If you keep a personal journal, write about your findings there.

♀ Exercise ♂
Cognitive Steps to Greater Sexual Freedom

Define Your Sexual Values for Yourself Ask yourself these questions: What do I think about female sexuality? How do I feel about having sex in a casual relationship? Is it okay for me to experience pleasure through sex? What do I need to feel turned on? How are my values different from those of my mother? My grandmothers? My sisters? My girlfriends?

Delve into Your Sexual History Ask your mother some general questions to find out about her attitudes about sex. Ask your female relatives and your girlfriends. Look for ideas that you inherited, which may no longer be appropriate to the woman you are. You don't have to get into the gory details; instead, you could ask general questions like, "Mom, what do you think about sexuality?"

Know What Turns You On and Accept It Forget about what the dominant culture says or what your parents defined as proper. You were made to have your body feel good. Claim the right (and the responsibility) to discover what feels good for you, before you ask someone else to please you sexually. If you don't know what you like, the exercises in this chapter will help you discover it.

Change Your Self-Talk The way you talk to yourself about who you are—statements such as "I shouldn't have these kinds of thoughts" or "He'll never want *me*"—will affect your orgasmic response. None of us can simply click into being proud, self-confident, relaxed, and shame-free in bed. To be those things takes listening to self-talk and changing negative beliefs to positive, self-affirming ones. Consider writing your positive affirmations down, many times, to help them sink in.

Sexual Self-Discovery: Opening to Yourself

If you are like most women in the baby boomer generation or the ones immediately following it, it's a safe bet that your mom never sat you down with a hand mirror and a speculum to teach you about the joy zones in your genitals. If you missed out on doing this in the forward-thinking women's groups in the 1970s, now is your chance to explore. Until you know where your pleasure zones are and how you like to be touched, and until you share that with your partner, how is he supposed to know?

Before I go into specifics, however, let's talk a bit about how to approach the exercises that follow. This will make all the difference in whether they are enjoyable and whether or not you feel motivated enough to follow through with them to achieve the pleasures of simultaneous and multiple orgasms.

Physically, remember to stay relaxed and to breathe deeply and evenly. Many of us are so used to holding our breath so we don't have to feel anything that we do it during sex—even though the whole point of sex is to feel, and to feel good. Breathing deeply and steadily brings you the oxygen necessary to build sexual arousal.

Here are the attitudes to cultivate as you progress through these exercises.

- **Do it for yourself.** Try to remember what it was like when you were very little and unselfconscious about exploring for pleasure. Tell yourself, "I want to do this for me. I am tired of not feeling what I want for myself. It doesn't matter what my partner, society, or anyone else wants. This is for me."

- **Center yourself before you begin.** Before each exercise, affirm: "I am doing this because I love myself. I know sex can be really good because sex has been around forever and ever. I want to make it better for myself."

- **Allow yourself to reconnect with the sensual inner child.** As little kids we were all very sexual, but that sexuality got taken out of us. Know that you can reconnect with that part of yourself again.

- **Set one goal only: to have a good time for yourself.** Explore with a sense of self-love and joy. Make it fun.

- **Make this exploration time a priority.** Schedule "dates" with yourself in your appointment book and keep them. If you don't schedule them, you will find that other things get in the way and you will never get around to them.

- **Drop self-criticism.** Be patient with yourself and self-loving. The learning curve can be slow. If it takes eight tries until you find your G-spot, so what? Don't give up if you don't see progress right away or if feelings of shame come up. Realize that self-critical messages often come from parents or teachers, and you are now grown-up enough to erase them. If you start thinking, "I'll never get this. Why am I having such a hard time?" know that your mind is playing an outdated tape, and substitute self-loving thoughts instead.

- **Be persistent.** If you are exploring a pleasure zone during an exercise and you don't feel anything, don't give up. Either you can sabotage yourself with "Oh, I don't feel anything," or you can help yourself with "I don't feel anything now, but I can if I refocus my mind and have a positive attitude." Then continue your exploration for a few minutes longer. You have to take the time to counter the old, faulty messages with your new beliefs that this touch will feel good. You may have to repeat your self-talk over and over, but persistence will pay off.

- **Keep your self-talk positive.** If you are not progressing as fast as you'd like, tell yourself, "I'm okay the way I am now. I'm just learning. I can take as much time as I want to learn." Keep the positive self-talk going throughout the day. If you find yourself being critical, refocus that talk also. An orgasm isn't just the result of physical stimulation but also how you feel about yourself that day. One thing I've found true for most of the women in my practice is that criticism can kill sexual pleasure. If your husband yells at you all morning, for instance, and then wants to have sex that night and bring you to orgasm, it's going to be really difficult. That's just not how we are wired.

- **Practice.** Be sure to practice the exercises and the self-talk for five to ten minutes, two times a week. You can practice more if you want, but this amount of time will be sufficient.

- **Do the self-exploration in a spirit of joy, discovery, and self-love.** Need I say more?

A Tour of Your Joy Spots

Throughout this exercise, remember to breathe and focus on your sensations. If you come to orgasm during these explorations, notice where your orgasm originates. Is it coming from inside your vagina or your clitoris, or is it a whole-body experience? Many times, a woman can stimulate different parts of her body but the orgasm will come from the same place. If you pay close attention, you'll soon discover what your body really likes and what it doesn't.

Before You Begin Set aside a quiet thirty minutes or so. Make sure you have privacy. Also make sure that your hands are very clean. Find a hand mirror and a light, natural oil that you like with enough viscosity so it won't dry out. (I recommend staying away from perfumed oils and petroleum jelly, because they can irritate this very sensitive skin, as well as KY jelly, which doesn't retain body warmth.)

The Exercise Let's locate the clitoris first. The clitoris is unique in that it has no function other than that of sexual pleasure. Using your hand mirror, notice how the inner lips of your vagina join at the bottom around the vaginal opening. At the top, they attach to the clitoris, a little nub with a hood of skin.

Now put your mirror away and try stroking and caressing around your clitoris. Different women like different kinds of touch. Some like a light touch directly on the clitoris. Others like to have the outer sides surrounding the clitoris stroked. Some prefer light strokes, others hard strokes. There is no formula for doing it right. I can't stress that enough: What's right is what you like.

Spend as much time as you want to exploring what feels good here. Remember to breathe, so you can really feel the sensations. Then, when you are ready (or you could choose to do this in a subsequent session), move outward toward your vaginal lips.

Some women, like me, prefer to stimulate inside the vagina. I like to start lightly on the outer side, stroking the labia, but I don't focus on the clitoris. I might even use my whole hand at first. Then, I'll move my hand inside the vagina. When you move into the vagina, you could use a finger or two, and you may or may not like to use oil. Explore and see for yourself.

As you are touching yourself, you may want to pay attention to what your brain likes to focus on when you are feeling aroused. Take your time. Enjoy yourself; refocus if your mind wanders.

Within the vagina itself is the G-spot, located on the front wall of your vagina, way up behind your pubic bone. It is often a firm spot with a ribbed texture. The G-spot may be a little tricky to find at first, but certain positions can make it easier. What works for me is getting on my hands and knees, with my shoulders on the bed and my butt high in the air. If you don't succeed at first, take comfort in the fact that many women have difficulty reaching it on their own, because it can be deep within the vagina. Before you go looking for your G-spot, be aware that many women don't feel comfortable going anywhere near their G-spot until they are sexually aroused and lubricated.

The most common way to locate your G-spot is to reach one or two fingers way up, back behind the pubic bone. Another way is to use a "gooseneck" or curved G-spot vibrator or soft rubber wand, which can reach further than your fingers. When you reach it, you may have an "Aha!" feeling or tingling, or you might feel pressure, as if you have to urinate.

Stimulating the G-spot can create intense arousal and trigger an orgasm from deep within the vagina. My G-spot orgasms set off muscle spasms much higher up than with clitoral orgasms. I feel the sensations deep in my vagina and in my thighs and belly. They feel almost like an ache, but in a delightful way. For me, the area keeps vibrating for ten minutes afterwards.

This G-spot is the source of the "gusher" or ejaculatory orgasm, so-called because some women do ejaculate fluid with them. You can bring a gusher about through masturbation, if you want to try something radically different. To be honest, not a whole lot is known about gusher-style orgasms. I find they are deeper and even more intense than regular G-spot orgasms. However, I'm not as crazy about these as G-spot orgasms because, once a gusher happens, I can't keep going. Most women find that their body needs a recovery period after these, just as a man does when he ejaculates, and that they are very sensitive and even a little sore.

Using Sex Toys

If you are learning how to become more orgasmic with a partner, there is one sex toy that can be a great help, and another that can impede your efforts. Let's talk about the latter first.

For now, say good-bye to your vibrator. Put it in the back of the drawer. The problem with a vibrator is that it offers very intense stimulation that a penis, mouth, or hand cannot duplicate. If you become accustomed to using that intensity of stimulation to reach orgasm, it will make it much more difficult for you to climax with a partner.

On the other hand, a dildo can be very useful. You can use it to train your muscles to spasm when an object, such as the penis, is inserted into the vagina. The nice thing about a dildo when you are discovering your sexuality is that you can take your time with it and go at your own pace. If you are learning solely with a partner, you end up worrying about his feelings or having an orgasm for him.

The exercises below all use a dildo. I suggest you find one that is pleasing to the eye. Make sure you choose one that you feel comfortable with—it's not good if you think, "Yuck, that's a dildo!" Many classy, reputable catalogues, such as the one from Good Vibrations of San Francisco, offer an appealing assortment of products. Consider choosing a toy that's fun and colorful, maybe bright orange or passion purple. And look for one that is specifically designed to stimulate your G-spot.

After you have done some initial exploring and chosen sexual aids that work for you, get ready to extend your orgasmic range! If you only have clitoral orgasms right now, you will soon learn to have vaginal and G-spot orgasms, with or without a partner. These exercises progress in several phases so that you can gradually build your skill. Remember to be patient and to enjoy each step of the way.

Ecstasy Training: Level 1

Practice these alone before you get together with your partner, progressing from having orgasms in ways that already work for you to having orgasms solely from the in-and-out stimulation of a dildo, like the thrusting of your lover. Try scheduling several private practice sessions for yourself each week, for as many weeks as it takes, until you are completely at ease with this.

♀ Exercise ♂
Vaginal Orgasms

A dildo that approximates the size and curvature of your partner's penis will help immeasurably, because it will get your muscles used to spasming when something that size is inserted into your vagina.

Before You Begin Secure thirty minutes of private time in a warm room, and center yourself with deep breathing. Caress your genitals lightly before masturbating, and make sure you have plenty of natural lubrication (or use a lubricant) before you begin using the dildo. During the exercise, try to work in some pelvic rolls and thrusts (see Chapter 4). Being aware of the sound of your own deep breathing can help you stay relaxed and feeling sexy.

Stage One Masturbate in a way that has worked for you in the past (if you have a past). When you are aroused and lubricated, insert the dildo (it's always wise to use a fresh condom on your dildo for hygiene purposes). You may want to hold it inside with one hand while you use the other hand to pleasure yourself. It may feel awkward at first, but experiment as much as you have to, to see what feels right. Remember your self-talk. Then, masturbate until you reach orgasm. Repeat this exercise, as you wish, over the next week.

Don't worry about doing more than this the first week or so. Allow yourself to get used to the feeling of having something inside you during arousal and orgasm. As orgasm approaches and you surrender to it, focus on the spasms in your vagina. If you can reach orgasm without fantasizing, don't fantasize. Focus completely on your exquisite physical sensations. If you can't reach orgasm without fantasizing, that's okay—go ahead and fantasize; eventually, you will want to get your mind into your body's sensations. Make note of what special physical movements or mental images seem to precipitate your orgasmic response. These will be very useful as simultaneous orgasm triggers when you get to Chapter 8, And Now, The Moment You've All Been Waiting For. If you don't orgasm right away, that's okay. If you hit what feels like an insurmountable roadblock, you may want to seek the assistance of a certified sex therapist.

Stage Two Once you get used to all of this, begin to experiment. See what happens when you squeeze your PC muscle around the dildo. Try squeezing during arousal, before orgasm, at the moment of orgasm. Try short, light squeezes and longer ones. What adds to your arousal? Be careful not to squeeze too much during one session or add squeezes too close to each other, as you'll get tense and reduce your arousal.

Do a week or so of these experimental sessions.

Stage Three When you are comfortable with all of the above (and it doesn't matter how many sessions it takes you to get comfortable—you only learn at a pace that comes naturally for you), try this next step.

After arousal, try moving the dildo in and out slowly and rhythmically. Remember to breathe, stay relaxed, and focus on the sensations in your vagina. If you have found the PC squeeze helpful during previous sessions, include it with this one. Try to be aware of the point of inevitability before climax. What sensations do you feel at that point? What feelings lead up to it?

Stage Four When you can identify your point of inevitability, try this during a session. When you are just about ready to come, stop any clitoral stimulation but continue to thrust the dildo in and out. Breathe and focus on your sensations as you do this. Reassure your body that everything is okay and give yourself permission to experience the orgasm in a new way. Continue to pleasure yourself with this in-and-out motion until you reach climax.

Stage Five As you continue these practice sessions for yourself, slowly decrease the amount of clitoral stimulation you need to reach orgasm. Take as much time as you need to get to the point where the dildo alone is enough to bring you to orgasm. You can use clitoral stimulation intermittently to get things going if you need to, but try not to depend on it for all your arousal. Fantasizing about making love to your partner, about having him move inside of you, will really help. This progression gets you to associate orgasm with the stimulation you receive from thrusting. Make a mental note of your orgasmic triggers as you did for the prior exercise.

G-Spot Orgasms

Now that you know where your G-spot is and what it feels like to stimulate it, here's something you can do to practice having a G-spot orgasm. Because these can bring very intense pleasure, you may need to will yourself to surrender to the feelings and open up to the intensity of sexual buildup until orgasmic release.

First, get a G-spot vibrator or a G-spot attachment for your vibrator. When you begin to pleasure yourself, use the lowest possible vibration. You may have to experiment to get the angle just right. Be aware of what angle feels good so that later you can most satisfyingly position yourself with your partner.

Be aware that G-spot stimulation sometimes results in "gushers," the female equivalent of an ejaculatory orgasm. The fluid of a gusher comes from the G-spot, and there can be a noticeable amount. If you're the kind of woman who has gusher orgasms regularly, you might want to put a large bath or beach towel on the bed. Also, be considerate of your partner during oral sex. Unfortunately, the lack of knowledge about gusher orgasms has scared some women away from the G-spot. Some women who had gusher orgasms thought that they had lost control and urinated (some had doctors who actually assured them that this is what happened), and they program themselves never to have such a humiliating experience again. Let me tell you that gusher orgasms are something to be proud of, not something to be ashamed of. If you can program yourself to stop having them, you can use your mind to release that inhibition, too.

Arousal Levels, Peaking, and Plateauing

We presented the concepts of arousal levels, peaking, and plateauing, along with related exercises for men, in Chapter 5. These techniques are absolutely necessary for ejaculatory control, a common challenge essentially unique to men. This material is less detailed for women because very few can be considered *prematurely orgasmic*, a rare situation meaning that they have one orgasm very rapidly following penetration, and then may continue having intercourse until their partner climaxes. If you fall into that category, these exercises may be of great value to you.

Indeed, you can learn to control and delay your own orgasmic response. However, since most women who are orgasmic are healthfully so, it is often not necessary or desirable to interfere with their normal pattern. On the other hand, women who will benefit significantly from learning to peak and plateau are those who sometimes find it difficult to orgasm or who are in a pattern of trying to get aroused and stimulated from ground zero to orgasm without interruption. Such a pattern can create pressure to orgasm in a certain manner and within a certain time frame, which makes it difficult if not impossible to come at all. Peaking and plateauing provide such a woman with an exhilarating array of options for arousal patterns and, when she desires a simultaneous orgasm, the ability to delay her orgasm if she is about to come and her partner is not quite ready.

Arousal Levels

The range of physical and psychological arousal has been discussed earlier in this chapter (Orgasm 101: The Act In All Its Varieties). We can distinguish arousal levels on a 1–10 scale. The extremes of 1 and 10 are easily identifiable: 1 means no arousal whatsoever, while 10 means you are orgasming. At levels 2 through 5, you feel the beginnings of sexual and emotional excitement, vaginal lubrication, muscle tension, increased breath intensity, and vaginal engorgement along with a possible swelling of your clitoris. Further up the scale at levels 6 through 9, all of the preceding features of arousal are more intense, possibly accompanied by facial flushing, shortness of breath, sweating, involuntary muscular and vaginal spasming, and pounding of the heart. In the 8–9 range you have the sense of orgasmic urgency that precedes the orgasm itself, and at 9+ a point of orgasmic inevitability is reached. In addition, each woman will have a set of unique, personal arousal experiences to add to the above list.

Peaking and Plateauing

Peaking is both the act of and the ability to have your arousal go up and down three or more arousal levels as defined above. This means, for example, that you can go up and down between levels 5 and 8, if you so desire, for an extended time.

A plateau is really a flattened out or extended peak. This means that you can hover in a narrow range of arousal for an extended time. The experiences of peaking, plateauing, and then orgasming (or not) can be mixed and matched. By mastering these abilities, you gain control over your own arousal levels and orgasmic releases, thereby increasing your sexual possibilities. As explained in Chapter 7, these techniques are also a way to become multiply orgasmic.

The Exercises

You should practice the following solo arousal awareness, peaking, and plateauing exercises using three different methods. First use hand self-stimulation. When that is working to your satisfaction, start using a dildo as the stimulation. Finally, practice using stimulation from your partner. All three methods produce essentially identical effects—with a few differences that are noted at the end.

Your objectives in this exercise are to:

- Develop an arousal awareness so you know approximately where on the 1–10 scale you are at any time.

- Learn to create both peaking and plateauing arousal patterns as often as you wish.

Arousal Awareness

You are probably already aware of your arousal, but not at a conscious level in terms of the 1–10 scale. Be sure you are familiar with the physical and psychological 1–10 scale arousal responses along with your personal arousal and orgasmic responses. Then, after self- or partner stimulation, make mental notes. Be particularly aware of what you feel at those higher arousal levels (7,8,9) and just prior to orgasm, and of what seems to trigger your orgasm.

♀ Exercise ♂
Peaking and Plateauing

Peaking will help you learn to bring your arousal level down three or four notches, and then restimulate yourself back up. Plateauing will allow you to stay aroused at a high level, with sustained stimulation, and keep yourself from coming if you so desire. Or you can keep returning to your plateau after a climax. You will do four basic things, alone or in combination, to create peaks and plateaus. Take about fifteen minutes every time you do these, and do them enough so that you have them down pat. You can end any exercise with an orgasm or not; it's your choice. The four basic procedures to use, while caressing and stimulating yourself in your favorite manner are:

- **PC Squeeze:** By squeezing your PC muscle, you can reduce your arousal level or keep it from escalating. One or two hard squeezes or several softer squeezes in succession will do.

- **Deep Breathing:** Deep breathing, fully and slowly into your stomach and chest, will also help bring down your arousal level.

- **Relaxing:** Relaxing you entire body, from the tip of your toes the top of your head, has the same effect as the above approaches.

- **Detumescing Strokes:** A detumescing stroke is one that travels away from your genitals. In general, any manual stroking in the direction of the genitals heighten arousal. Conversely, any stroking away from the genitals has the opposite effect. By caressing your legs up from your knees, or down from your lower chest, towards your vagina you will become more aroused. The reverse effect occurs when stroking away from the genitals.

If you try the above techniques with a partner, keep in mind that he will be reading and practicing his own version of peaking and plateauing exercises for men. Some of them involve partner participation, so you can set time aside to do your partner exercises with each other.

One of the partner exercises is a genital caress, in which each of you will do some sustained caressing while the other goes through his training. You can use manual or oral stimulation, or a combination of the two, while you practice.

Make a date with your partner to do this exercise. Let him know that it is an exercise in which he will be the active partner caressing your genitals while you practice certain arousal techniques. Suggest that it may be a good time for him to practice those exercises he also needs to do with a partner. If that is not appropriate, arrange the time simply to do yours. Set aside at least thirty minutes of relaxed quality time, free of interruptions from telephones and children. Create a comfortable ambiance in terms of lighting, temperature, and music. Before you start, demonstrate and explain to him how to do the detumescing stroke away from your genitals. Suggest the manner in which you want to be caressed: manually, orally, or both. It is up to you to tell him what kind of stimulation you desire, and when you want it increased, decreased, or changed.

Do a few minutes of hugging and holding each other. Lie on your back and take a signal breath to let your body know you are ready to begin. Then, have him begin pleasuring you with caresses and stimulation. Remember to breathe, relax, and focus. At times, you may want to show him exactly how you want to be touched. If he is doing something you don't like, tell him that also. Keep in mind that he is not primarily responsible for your arousal, you are.

Let your body succumb to the pleasures it is receiving. Allow your arousal to build up naturally to level 7 or higher. Now start to practice peaking. On your own, do some PC squeezes, deep breathing, and full body relaxation. You may also ask your partner to stop or decrease the stimulation and perhaps do some detumescing strokes. In that manner, drop your arousal down to about 5. Then allow it to build up again. Do the peaks several times. If you are still in the mood, you may practice plateauing. If not, you can do it next time by starting off with plateaus or doing just one preliminary peak. To plateau, allow your arousal to build up once again to level 7 or higher. While the stimulation continues at equal intensity, keep your arousal level steady by using the same techniques you used for the peaks. You can now stop and slowly come down, orgasm, or do some more peaks—whatever feels best.

Have patience with yourself and with your partner. Luxuriate in the time you spend on this exercise.

Female Ejaculatory Orgasms and Childbirth

What could nature possibly have had in mind by giving a woman the ability to ejaculate? We know why men ejaculate, but why do women? And why is it that this kind of orgasm often makes a woman feel so satisfied that she's ready to go without sex for a while?

Michael found, quite by accident, that some women only experience the gusher phenomenon during childbirth. In 1989, he did hypnosis regression with a client who was easily capable of clitoral orgasms but who had difficulty with vaginal orgasms. When he asked her, under hypnosis, whether she had ever experienced a G-spot orgasm, she said yes. When he asked her when, she talked about the last few minutes during the birth of both her children.

The woman indicated that during her gusher experiences she felt some dull discomfort, mixed with very soothing sensations in the vaginal area as the baby was starting to emerge. As the baby's head came out, she felt her vagina spasm, and an intense rush of fluid pulsed and spurted as the child came free.

As he continued to work with her, she was able to bring her subconscious memory into conscious thought. She became very aware of her potential for intense pleasure. That, along with the sex therapy exercises detailed in this book, allowed her to experience vaginal orgasms with her lover. (As an interesting aside, during childbirth this woman had used the Lamaze method, which includes deep breathing and focusing techniques similar to what we teach to help people become more sexually responsive.)

There are many reasons why nature would have paired gusher orgasms with childbirth. The intense pleasure gusher helps offset the pain of childbirth (sexual stimulation causes the release of endorphins into the body), and the fluid helps sterilize the birth canal for the baby and aids its progress through it. The fact that a gusher orgasm totally satiates a woman may also compensate for the fact that she probably won't be having intercourse for a while, as she recovers from the birth. Michael and I also wonder if it enhances the process of bonding with the new baby. If this is true, it contradicts conventional "wisdom" that female sexual sensations have no value other than pleasure.

If you are pregnant or are a mother who has had difficulty with orgasm, consider the connection between G-spot sensation, gusher orgasms, and childbirth. You can definitely use the childbirth experience to anchor in these kinds of vaginal orgasms by bringing the subconscious memory into consciousness.

Becoming Orgasmic with Your Partner: Tips, Positioning, and Technique

Now that you've spent some time giving yourself loving, sensuous, much-deserved attention and—I hope—discovering new ways to be pleasured, you may feel ready and excited to share your discoveries with your lover. You may also feel a little anxious or nervous about doing so. Although you have learned to relax and let go alone, will you be able to do so as easily with your lover? Now is the time to remember that sexual union is not a contest. Sexual union, with all its pleasures, is a journey. So, savor each step, and don't rush things or raise pressuring expectations.

Before you begin the partner exercises, ask your partner how he feels about trying mutual, non-goal-oriented sexual exploration. I'll bet he's game. I've found during years of sex counseling that, while men are naturally oriented toward orgasm, they really enjoy and are turned on by their partner's interest in exploration—and the spontaneous, unforced arousal that it uncovers.

If your partner is hesitant about trying these new things, he may be feeling performance anxiety, or wondering if your need to experiment means you find him inadequate as a lover. Reassure him. Let him know you are excited about being with him and that what you desire is for both of you to learn more about each other. Reassure him that the idea is to have fun. Remind him that this is a journey you never had a previous chance to take. Remember, there's no pressure on either of you to achieve anything.

Here are three love games to get you started. They will help you become generally orgasmic with your partner. Later exercises will work on creating specific kinds of orgasms together.

♀ Exercise ♂
Fake It till You Make It

"Hey, wait a minute! This book is on how to have great orgasms, and you're asking me to fake it?" Don't worry! I'm not asking you to fake it to boost your partner's ego. This exercise is about simulation and experience, to bring you into a new frame of mind. Instead of wondering what it's like to push yourself over the edge, you will have what we call a simulated orgasmic experience, with the full understanding and cooperation of your partner. That lifts the pressure. Now you no longer have to focus on having an orgasm, because you will be acting as if you are.

The Exercise The next time you are really aroused, imagine what it would be like to have an orgasm. Then move, sound, and talk as if you are having that orgasm right at that moment. You might find this easiest if you are in a position on top of your partner. That way, you can have the freedom to move so that his penis is pleasuring *you*. The idea is to do it the way you like it, whether slow and sensuous or fast and furious. The exercise is also wonderful for freeing you from any inhibitions you feel about moaning, making noise, or moving vigorously. If your partner changes the pace, gently remind him that in this exercise it is important that you set the pace. You can try different sounds and movements on for size, and make them yours—whether you identify with Jane Seymour or Madonna.

A significant number of women find that they spontaneously have a vaginal orgasmic response and release when doing this exercise. The simple act of giving themselves permission to act and feel this way allows it to happen. But the main advantage of this exercise is that you get to sample from a range of sexual expression that you normally don't allow yourself to feel. The only thing you are meant to do is enjoy the process.

♀ Exercise ♂
Towel over His Face

Like all partner exercises, this one requires permission from your partner. During this session, you will make love to your partner while he's lying on his back, with a light towel over his face. What this does is depersonalize your partner so you can experience his body solely for your pleasure. Some women think that this sounds radical, and lots of people object to it at first—until they understand the point.

While you are making love with your partner, two relationships are happening simultaneously. One is your relationship with him, of course, and the other is one that often gets ignored: your sexual relationship with yourself. In order to have a strong sexual relationship with your partner, your sexual relationship with yourself has to be strong. With this exercise, you depersonalize an intimate act to make it more personal for you. It is an incredibly potent reinforcement of the concept that you are responsible for your own orgasmic reactions. If you are the type who lets your partner's responses cue your behavior, this exercise trains you to look to your own pleasure as a new reference point.

The Exercise Imagine your partner as a sumptuous, seven-course gourmet meal to be relished with gusto. While he is lying on the bed, straddle him in such a way that gives you complete access to his body. You might decide to rub his nose, toes, fingers, hands, and penis and rub them with your face, neck, nipples, labia, clitoris, belly button, fingertips—whatever feels delicious. You can stroke and tease his penis, kiss soft or hard, lick or suck. Anything goes, provided you aren't causing your partner pain or discomfort. He is not to talk during this exercise.

Don't worry about your partner—I pretty much guarantee he is going to have a good time, and you are not responsible for his response. Focus on what it feels like to give yourself over to seeking pleasure without worrying about how someone else feels. Many women find this, in itself, to be highly arousing.

♀ Exercise ♂
Distract the Distraction

As Michael and I have noticed, some women become so anxious about whether or not they are going to climax that instead of surrendering to their body's natural orgasmic response, they shut it down. Their anxiety causes a fight or flight response, which distracts people from the arousal-building pleasure of lovemaking. We could simply tell you not to become anxious, but that presents a classic dilemma: tell people not to think something, and all of a sudden that's all they can think about. That's how we came up with this exercise.

The idea here is to take your mind away from anxiety by forcing you to focus on something else. It's sneaky, I admit, but it really works.

The Exercise To begin, find a tape or CD of music you really hate—whether it's rap, country & western, heavy metal, or 1950s rock, whatever. Just make sure the music makes you squirm. Put on a pair of headphones and listen to the music while your partner is caressing you, stimulating you, and making love to you. Keep the music at a level that doesn't burst your eardrums but is loud enough to be very annoying.

The point of this exercise is that your mind now has to fight off a kind of noise it hates, something much more annoying than personal fear. You will have no choice but to be in the here and now, engaged with all your senses, instead of worried and fearful, thinking of the future. This leaves your body free to respond to the stimulation it is receiving. Higher levels of arousal are now possible, because you're not continually monitoring yourself. After a while switch roles and have your partner select some music he hates and put on the headphones.

Orgasm du Jour—Together!

The previous exercises were designed to help you become more comfortable being fully orgasmic with your partner. If you'd like to achieve a particular kind of orgasm with him, have different types of orgasm in one lovemaking session, or blend different types of orgasms into one—the sky is the limit!

Each kind of orgasm feels different. Alicia Snelen, who has worked as a sexual surrogate in our office, finds that clitoral orgasms tend to create very localized, intense contractions in her vaginal area, while G-spot orgasms send waves of pleasure throughout her body. She can even mix and match orgasms.

Alicia explains what she frequently does with a partner: "We will start out petting and there will be some oral sex. I might have one orgasm through oral sex, and then when we have intercourse, I have a few orgasms with vaginal stimulation and sometimes an ejaculatory response with G-spot stimulation."

Again, positioning will help vary stimulation, arousal responses, and the types of orgasm you can have. Here are some guidelines.

♀ Exercise ♂
The High Rider

As I've said before, an estimated 50 percent of woman in the United States are unable to reach orgasm through intercourse. If you have practiced the exercises above, you are likely to be in the lucky 50 percent. But you should know this: failure to have an orgasm during intercourse does not automatically mean that there is something wrong with his lovemaking or wrong with you. Some women have more sensitivity in their clitoris and may need clitoral stimulation during intercourse to help them reach orgasm. Following is a wonderful position that will help your lover provide this.

The Exercise Have him spread and hold your legs open with his legs and ankles. If it feels good for both of you, he can also hold your wrists, palms up, above your head. Then have him push his body further up on you than usual. We call this the High Rider. It gives excellent clitoral stimulation and will also create some wonderful feelings in the ridge surrounding the head of your lover's penis. For a variation, try this while you both do pelvic rolls and thrusts, in the same direction, at the same speed. This is called the coital alignment technique.

"I find that pretty much any position works for the vaginal orgasm," says Alicia. "I have a small repertoire. Usually, my partner is on top and I wrap my legs around his waist, which is a little less direct for the G-spot. Or, my legs are around his shoulders, or my knees are bent up around his shoulders. I also like 'doggy style,' either with me lying on my stomach or just kneeling." She adds, "Whatever the position, I like to be physically comfortable, so that I can maintain it longer. It boils down to this: I like to focus the sexual energy into our genitals as much as possible. If I have to exert a lot of energy to support myself or maintain a position that's awkward, it's harder to really enjoy the sexual activity."

The Female Orgasm In Literature

Our denials came closer and closer together as he found a hard, driving rhythm that satisfied both of us. I lost all sense of place and time and even of self as he drove into me and drove himself, and me, finally, over the brink into a fierce, all-consuming orgasm, with a final shout, in which our two voices mingled.

—Lisa Tuttle, "The Story of No,"
from *The Mammoth Book of Erotica*, ed. Maxim Jakubowski
(New York: Caroll and Graf, 1994)

And then they both began to move again, interlocking, cock and cunt, and nothing else in the world mattering. She came with a shudder that shook her whole body and released another scream from her that scarcely seemed human. Everything released as she screamed and came; she also peed, and was embarrassed and apologized....

He held her to him even as his cock grew soft and curled away from her. "I'll never leave you," he said, "never."

—Erica Jong, *How to Save Your Own Life*
(New York: Holt Rinehart, 1977)

As he began to move, in the sudden helpless orgasm there awoke in her strange thrills rippling inside her. Rippling, rippling, rippling, like a flapping overlapping of soft flames, soft as feathers, running to points of brilliance, exquisite, exquisite and melting her all molten inside. It was like bells rippling up and up to a culmination. She lay unconscious of the wild little cries she uttered at the last.

—D. H. Lawrence, *Lady Chatterly's Lover*
(New York: Grove Press, 1969)

We have seen that the act of love requires of woman profound self-abandonment—she bathes in a passive languor; with closed eyes, anonymous, lost, she feels as if borne by waves, swept away in a storm, shrouded in darkness of the flesh, of the womb, of the grave. Annihilated, she becomes one with the Whole, her ego is abolished. But when the man moves from her, she finds herself back on earth, on a bed, in the light; she again has a name, a face: she is one vanquished, prey, object.

—Simone de Beauvoir, *The Second Sex*
(New York: Vintage Books, 1989)

What You Both Should Know about G-Spot Orgasms

Some women can have multiple G-spot orgasms or have a series of orgasms, some of which result from clitoral stimulation, some from vaginal stimulation, and some from G-spot stimulation. You may find that intensity of pleasure takes some getting used to.

Be sure to let your partner know that you first need to be aroused and wet before you want G-spot stimulation. Says Alicia, "I don't like to have it touched too much until I am aroused because it is easily irritated. It's like having someone touch a full bladder. If we are starting to play around a little bit and he's putting his finger inside of me, I'll tell my partner to take it easy and go slow. Once I warm it up, then I can start moving and thrusting and can receive more intense stimulation."

To help your partner find your G-spot, have him insert his middle finger into your vagina. Tell him to hook his finger up and forward and imagine that the G-spot is on the back side of the clitoris. One way he can do this is by putting his thumb on your clitoris and trying to touch his thumb with his finger, as if he were making the "OK" sign. He will know he's found it when he reaches a fleshy, textured area that he can roll his finger around. If he puts sustained pressure on it, he will feel a pulsing.

There are various ways your lover can stimulate your G-spot, and intercourse is one of them. The three best intercourse positions for G-spot stimulation are the following:

- Woman on top, so you can guide the angle, intensity, direction, and speed of thrusting.

- Rear entry, because the angle it creates between the penis and the vagina gives deeper penetration (this is even better if you are on your hands and knees).

- Man on top, with your legs up over your partner's shoulders and your bottom slightly off the ground or mattress. Your partner should lean far forward, so he can rest on his elbows; you may find that a pillow or two under your butt is a big help.

When you are ready to try G-spot orgasms during intercourse, try these variations. To prepare yourself for each of them, have your lover finger you during foreplay or do it yourself. If he isn't very agile at reaching your G-spot, adjust yourself so that his finger is at just the right angle, and move in a way that feels good. You may need to do this at first to teach him where and how you want your G-spot to be stroked.

The first time you try for one, have him enter you with you on top. This is best to start with, because it lets you control the timing and the stimulation. Move in a way that uses his erection to stimulate your G-spot. Call into play any kind of erotic stimulation that works for both of you—whether it's making sounds, sharing love talk, or touching each other in particular ways. You will experience yourself as more vulnerable when your intercourse position shifts to side-to-side, having him on top, or having him enter you from behind. When he is the more active partner, you may need to guide him more so he can give you the stimulation you need.

If his penis has a typical curve or upward bend, it may be possible for him to feel your G-spot on the head of his penis. Tell him when he makes contact with it so he can take a minute to register what it feels like and where it is. Then have him move *very* slowly back and forth on the G-spot or flick his PC muscle when he makes contact with the it. This will give you additional stimulation by giving the G-spot an up-and-down friction in addition to the in-and-out movement of thrusting.

The Next Step

You have taken in quite a bit of information in this chapter, and covered a lot of sexual ground. There's no reason to rush through any exercise; in fact, repeating them will reinforce them for you. Take your time and explore your sexual nuances. You can only learn at your own pace. Enjoy the process of becoming orgasmic, and enjoy what it does to the entirety of your relationship with yourself and your lover. (See the Appendix for a visual conception of your improvement.)

When you feel grounded and powerful in your orgasmic possibilities, move on to the next chapter, in which Michael and I explain how you and your partner can share the terrific experience of multiple orgasms.

> ## A Word To Men
>
> Learning to be immodest and orgasmic can be an anxiety-provoking process for your partner. Here are a few ways you can be supportive and helpful:
>
> 1. Help her get " alone and privacy time" to do her solo exercises. This includes freedom from household chores and interruptions by children.
>
> 2. Come to the partner exercises with a spirit of play and learning and free of expectations. If she needs you to stop or change, do as she asks.
>
> 3. This is a temporary phase which is leading to better and better experiences for you both.
>
> 4. You can concentrate on your own pleasure and arousal levels as well so this can be good practice.
>
> 5. While growing up, women often get faulty messages about their sexuality. Encourage her to "march to her own drummer."

Notes

1. Gina Ogden, Ph.D., *Women Who Love Sex* (New York: Pocket Books, 1994), 128–159.

Chapter 7
Maximizing Your Pleasure: Mastering the Multiple Orgasm

> The orgasm reminds me of a dam breaking ... the best part is the continuing waves of build-up and release during multiple orgasms.
>
> —An anonymous woman, in *The Hite Report*

It is no secret that women are capable of having one orgasm after another after another, as closely spaced as pearls on a necklace, but it may surprise you that men have this potential, too. We rather like the fact that nature is so evenhanded in this regard. While it's true that women find multiple orgasms much easier to learn than men, we assure you that the steps outlined in this chapter will take any man there, if he has the patience. Practicing these solo and partner exercises—enjoyable in themselves—will have a stupendous payoff!

Before going into the exercises, we'd like to talk a bit about the emotional responses that multiple orgasms can bring up. Some men are surprised to find they experience a subtle fear when their lover becomes multiorgasmic. This may not happen, or it may come up in ways that the two of you don't immediately recognize. As you begin exploring the new, intimate territory of the following pages, be aware. Fear and envy can muddy the waters between you at a time when you should be drawing closer. If you don't deal with these feelings consciously, they can spark sabotaging behaviors and will prevent you from realizing your full potential for sexual pleasure as a couple.

The social taboos for women who claim and exercise their full sexual powers are still very strong, although often hidden. The fear, ridiculous once it is exposed, is that a woman who takes full enjoyment in her sexuality is a threat to men and organized society. Once she knows the pleasure available to her, exemplified by multiple orgasm, she will become insatiable. She won't remain faithful to any man, and she may even lure other woman's husbands into sexual trysts. This fundamental fear underlies several taboos in many cultures. You and your beloved participate in the collective consciousness where such taboos are lodged. One or both of you may find, on introspection, that you share these beliefs—that they are part of the faulty learning you inherited. If you can become conscious of these beliefs, you can work together to transform them into beliefs that fully support each of you in reclaiming full sexual power. You both need to feel comfortable with female sexual power, on all levels, to experience the heights of pleasure available to you through physical intimacy.

That said, let's look at what it takes for a woman to become multi-orgasmic. Men, you should read this section before moving on to your section on male multiple orgasm in the second part of this chapter. Women, you should read the section on men after you have finished with your section.

As you both have done with the program throughout this book, set aside some time alone and some time together for these sexually pleasing practice sessions.

The Multiple Orgasm for Women

Before you begin, there are a few things you should know. The first, believe it or not, is that multiple orgasm is not necessarily the ultimate sexual experience for every woman. Some prefer one major orgasm rather than many smaller ones, as they are so supersensitive after that one orgasm that they are ready to stop. Other women orgasm like operatic sopranos—just when you think they're going to run out of steam, they build to fever pitch again. Each and every woman is unique, and there is no better or best way to sexual fulfillment. One of the great thrills of exploring your sexuality is to find out what you're all about.

The second thing you should know is that even members of the professional sex therapy community can't entirely agree on what exactly multiple orgasm is. *Our* definition is simple: multiple orgasm for women is a lot like peaking and plateauing. You can bring yourself to an arousal level of 9 or 10 and have a really powerful orgasm; or you can peak, allow your arousal to drop back down to 5, 6, or 7, relax into orgasm at the lower level of intensity, and begin building toward your next one. If you allow your arousal to move up and down like this, you can have one orgasm after another without moving into the refractory, or resting, period. (In comparison, a man moves into the refractory period when his erection subsides.)

How difficult is it to have multiple orgasms when you're already orgasmic? To tell you the truth, not very! If you can tap into that place where you connect with the deep and primal wellsprings of desire and allow yourself enough pleasurable stimulation, all you need to do is surrender. If none of this comes easily, it just means you have to strip away the barriers you (and society) have erected between you and your natural sexual instincts. Chapter 6 discussed how to do this in depth; if you need reinforcement, revisit that chapter from time to time.

Sometimes the hard part is allowing yourself to become stimulated enough. Many women we've seen in our practice have never felt fully aroused. This is not unusual, since so many of us were taught to "turn it off" until we were married or older. After all those years of suppression, it is not always easy to turn it back on. It might feel funny or weird when you first try. Keep reminding yourself, though, that there are no right or wrong feelings. Although you might get uncomfortable or scared about feeling aroused, this will lessen over time. In fact, over time, you will feel great!

For other women, full stimulation is no problem. Their challenge is learning how to completely surrender once they reach the point of inevitability. If this describes you, then the following five key elements will help you overcome this tendency. We suggest you write down these key points and post them where you can glance at them whenever you feel frustrated.

- **Breath.** Are you breathing? Take slow, deep, relaxing breaths. Holding your breath at any time keeps you tense.

- **State of relaxation.** Is your body relaxed? Take a mental inventory of your tension. The more you can let go, the easier it is to *relax into orgasm*. (Anita first heard that phrase from her mentor and teacher, the late Barbara Roberts, and she is still in awe of how a statement so simple can be so effective.)

- **Patience.** Are you being patient with yourself? Many of us have an internal clock that allows us only a certain amount of time to complete an exercise, even when it involves sex. Let go of your internal clock and allow yourself to follow a more natural timetable.

- **Internal congruence.** Sure, your conscious intent is to experience simultaneous orgasm, but is an inner part of you holding back? Learning new things or challenging the status quo can be scary. Courage is not being unafraid; it's feeling the fear and doing it anyway. So be courageous! You're a pioneer entering new territory.

- **Self-talk.** We achieve maximum functioning when our self-talk is loving and nonjudgmental. Be aware of your internal conversations, and continue making them positive and self-affirming.

♀ Exercise ♂
Sensate Focus in Service of the Multiple Orgasm

When you are ready to begin your exploration of multiple orgasm, set aside a time and place where you can be alone for more than an hour. For women one of the keys to having multiple orgasms is spending lots of time getting aroused and staying aroused without reaching climax. If you haven't felt very sexual lately or don't have much time to, it's important that you not pressure yourself. Let your feelings emerge as they are.

Before You Begin Prepare the room by locking the door, turning off the phone, and doing whatever you need to be undisturbed. You might want to set the mood with seductive music and candles or incense. Or, try reading a bit of erotica. Do you know what really turns you on? Don't dismiss erotica if you haven't tried it. (See the *Resources* section for ideas.)

If it is difficult for you to relax and let go of the day, begin with one of the progressive relaxation exercises in Chapters 3 and 4. If you are a veteran relaxer, take a few deep, relaxing breaths until you feel centered and open. When you are ready, take a signal breath.

The Exercise Use your hands to explore and arouse yourself the way you like best. Focus on your sensations—be present in the here and now. If your mind wanders away from your sensations, bring it back, again and again if you have to. As you caress your breasts, stimulate your clitoris, and bring yourself to a high level of arousal, continue taking deep breaths to relax deeper and deeper.

Allow yourself to surrender to the sensations. When your arousal reaches level 7 or 8, squeeze your PC muscle or stop stimulation for a while to bring your arousal down to level 4 or 5. Take slow, relaxing breaths at the same time.

Start stimulation again, peaking at 7 or 8, stopping, and dropping back to level 5 or 6. In this way, you are learning to prolong your arousal without becoming too sensitive to feel pleasured. Stay focused on your arousal and your body's response. Smother yourself with loving attention.

After peaking a while, get ready to build to climax. You might want to fantasize about your partner thrusting inside of you, over and over, or about being a voyeur looking at other couples in erotic embrace, as in the literature you read.

Unlike previous exercises, this time when you come close to orgasm, relax your PC completely. Don't tighten it. Feel your orgasmic response.

After you climax, take slow, deep, relaxing breaths. Be aware of what you are feeling and your overall level of arousal.

If you feel too sensitive to receive direct sexual stimulation again, wait a few moments. (If you are highly sensitive, see the Peaking Variation below.) If not, begin caressing yourself again, and repeat the process above until you bring yourself to orgasm.

Here are satisfying variations you might want to try in this or later sessions.

Self-Reflection Variation If you are visually oriented, pleasure yourself in front of a full-length mirror. Watch your body and vagina change with arousal and climax. Notice how you flush with desire and how being aware of your desire can arouse you more.

PC Squeeze Variation Instead of relaxing your PC muscle just before orgasm, try squeezing it. Experiment with a long, hard squeeze and a few light squeezes. Some women find this heightens their sexual response.

Peaking Variation If you are too sensitive to receive touch after an orgasm, try peaking at lower levels before building to a big climax or several small ones in rapid succession. (We teach men how to do something similar so they don't have a premature ejaculation.)

To peak, let your arousal build to a level of 7 or 8, then squeeze your PC muscle or stop stimulation until your arousal level drops to level 4 or 5. Take slow, relaxing breaths. Then start stimulation again, peaking at level 7 or 8, stopping, and dropping to level 5 or 6. This is how to prolong your arousal without getting too sensitive. Have fun with this, and enjoy the waves of arousal.

When you're ready for climax, let yourself open, open, open as you relax into orgasm. Don't force or push for it; just notice what happens. After a while, you will "know" what to do next to deepen your pleasure.

Once you begin to have multiple orgasms, you won't forget how to have them. The brain and body have amazing memories. Trust yourself to be able to repeat the process. And don't forget to remind yourself in your daily life of the five key points we listed above.

Enjoying Multiple Orgasms with Your Partner

When you are confident in your ability to have multiple orgasms alone, get ready to bring them about together with your lover. The experience alone is sexually powerful, but with a lover it becomes truly magical. If the two of you haven't had multiple orgasms before, be prepared for this watershed experience.

Let your partner know if you feel vulnerable and if you need to be reassured of his love. It is difficult to do these exercises if you don't feel loved and respected or loving and respectful of your partner. If you are upset with him, wait until you have resolved the issue before reaching for this intimate encounter. It can be impossible to switch gears if either of you has bad feelings about the relationship.

♀ Exercise ♂
Practicing with Your Partner

Set aside quality time with your partner, time when you are relaxed but not tired. Take a few moments to set the mood. Make sure the temperature is comfortable. Undress each other, if that turns you on.

Tell your partner that you need him to be the active partner during this exercise.

The Exercise Ease into intimacy and arousal by caressing your partner in a sensate focus way. Lie on your back, in a comfortable way, with your partner sitting next to you, facing you, near enough to comfortably stroke and caress your vagina. Take a signal breath to let your body know you are ready to begin. Then, have your partner begin pleasuring you with caresses and manual or oral stimulation. Relax, breathe, and focus.

If you like, show him exactly how you like to be touched. Remember, he is not responsible for your arousal—you are. If there is something you would like him to do or not do, you need to let him know.

Let your body fall into the pleasure it is receiving. Let your arousal build to a nice, high peak. When it hits level 8 or 9, let yourself orgasm, or at least plateau. Then, take a big, deep breath.

At this point, many women like to kiss, hug, and talk intimately. As your arousal subsides, stay focused on your pleasure. Don't let your mind shift gears, and don't focus on pleasuring your mate. Since most women don't need a long refractory period, have your partner begin sensuously caressing you again. Have him start softly, and see what type of touch you like now—softer or harder, gentler or faster.

Repeat the process as many times as you like, climbing to a full climax or peaking at lower arousal levels.

Most importantly, have patience with yourself and your partner. Be luxurious in the time you spend with this exercise. You may want to do this exercise a number of times to develop your orgasmic capacity and to discover the stroking and pacing that works best for you.

♀ Exercise ♂
Multiple Orgasms with Intercourse

This is the same exercise as the previous one, but it's done together with your lover during intercourse. He will need to be able to peak and control his ejaculation to sustain himself during this exercise (suggest Chapter 5 to him if he hasn't worked through the program already). Alternatively, he can combine manual and oral stimulation with intercourse, so he doesn't overstimulate himself. Since this exercise is for you, make sure you spend enough time focusing on your pleasure. Let him be responsible for himself.

If the reality of multiple orgasms feels far away the first few times you try this exercise, try the Fake It till You Make It approach (see Chapter 6, page 136), in which you act orgasmically when you begin to feel your highest level of arousal. Tell your partner first that this is what you will do, so he can help you. Go into it with the kind of confidence you would have if you had multiple orgasms every day. Usually, pretending and practicing helps your body get it, and what begins as fake orgasms trigger what become real ones.

♀ Exercise ♂
Ask Your Partner for More Support

Remember when we said that you are responsible for your own orgasm? Well, that is correct, but it is great to get a little help from your lover.

Throughout this program, you have been discovering and developing your own sexual style, so right about now is a good time to ask for what you want—and get what you need. What is your sexual style? Do you like romance? Do you enjoy being seduced? Do you like a rough-and-ready approach? There are a variety of ways your partner can help engage you sexually and prolong your pleasure so you experience enough stimulation to set off a wonderful string of orgasms.

The following are some of our favorite techniques. Play around with them to see what you enjoy.

- **Set the mood together.** If you are a good match, he might be turned on by the same ambiance that works for you, so indulge yourself. Or, create a setting that he never would have thought of and see what happens! Perhaps your preferences run toward soft music and bubble baths. Maybe you both like loud rock and strobe lights better. What you choose doesn't matter—just make sure it's something you like.

- **Ask for romantic talk.** Do you like being told how much he enjoys touching you? Let him know (offer him a reward if he's not prone to do this). If he's the strong and silent type don't be bashful about giving him sample lines or some kind of coaching first. Some men don't know how to think this way. They've never been taught and it doesn't come naturally.

- **Tell him you want him to growl and talk dirty.** Do you like being told what he wants from you, what he's going to do to you, or what turns him on? If so, let him know. What do you find erotic? How can you inspire him to meet your desires in this way?

- **Take him on a "touch tour" of your body.** Show him what you like and where you like it. Soft caresses, light kisses, a strong grasp—all can feel good at different times, in different ways. Once he knows, he can incorporate the kinds of touch that particularly turn you on!

- **Adjust the lighting.** Does dimming the lights make you amorous, or do you like the energy of watching each other? Do you enjoy the soft glow of candlelight or the velvet of moonlight? Make your love light the way you like it best.

Are you getting some ideas? There are an infinite number of ways you can make lovemaking a whole body, sensually rich experience for yourself. Just remember to express your needs in a positive way and invite your partner into the process. Making him feel like he's been clueless in the past won't put him in the mood to please you, and you may regret you even asked.

The Multiple Orgasm for Men

Countless men have envied women's ability to have multiple orgasms. Most men feel a steady building of arousal to the point of inevitability, then a powerful, intense sensation of orgasm during ejaculation, and that's it. If a man wants to come again, he must wait out his refractory period (the physiological lag time between erections), work up another erection, and start lovemaking all over again. Refractory periods vary in length from minutes to a day or more. Some men can maintain at least a partial erection after ejaculation and continue thrusting while working up to another orgasm. A few men, on their own, discover how to experience the intensely pleasurable sensation of orgasm without ejaculation or losing their erection. But for most men, separating orgasm and ejaculation requires instruction and practice.

First, let's be clear on the difference between orgasm and ejaculation, and why that difference is important. Most people equate the two, but they are actually separate events that usually occur simultaneously. To have multiple orgasms, a man must learn to "split" orgasm from ejaculation.

An ejaculation is simply the buildup and release of sexual tension localized directly in the genital area: After sufficient stimulation, the point of inevitability is reached, and a pleasurable pulsing and pumping sensation is felt as semen is expelled. An orgasm, on the other hand, is a buildup and release of tension throughout the entire body, accompanied by uncontrolled spasms, guttural utterances, rapid heartbeat, and breathing. While it is typical to have an orgasm and ejaculation at the same time, it is also possible to have an orgasm without ejaculating (and vice versa).

Men lose their erection and enter the refractory period only as a result of an ejaculation—not orgasm. So, if you reach orgasm without ejaculating, your erection will continue. This makes sense in an evolutionary context: ejaculation propagates the species, not orgasm. This process of nonejaculatory orgasms can go on indefinitely, until an ejaculation occurs or you simply decide that you've had enough and want to stop.

The ability to distinguish between orgasm and ejaculation, and to experience them separately, requires a heightened awareness of your arousal level and firm PC muscle control. Once you've mastered your PC muscle enough to control how long you last, you can learn to use your PC to separate orgasm from ejaculation—and once you can do this, multiple orgasms will be yours, too! If you have been doing the peaking exercises faithfully and exercising your PC muscle daily, you should be able to identify your various arousal levels on the 1 to 10 scale. To perfect the timing necessary for multiple orgasms, you need to be aware of your physiology.

Male ejaculation occurs in two phases: emission and expulsion. These two phases happen very close together, with the whole process taking only a few seconds. During emission, semen moves from the testicles to the penis via a tube called the *vas deferens*, while muscles near the prostate gland begin to spasm. The semen then collects in an area at the base of the penis called the urethral bulb. During expulsion, the PC muscle spasms rhythmically, pushing the semen up and out through the penis. This is usually an involuntary process, but with your newfound PC muscle control, it can become voluntary. By controlling the expulsion phase, you can experience the sensations of orgasm—the heart-racing, deep-breathing, muscle-spasm feeling of release—without ejaculating. And you can do it again and again.

The following exercises will help you practice and perfect your timing for multiple orgasms. Remember, be patient while you are learning. Once you've got it, you will really have it. You will only improve with time as you hone and refine your technique. As your body becomes accustomed to this new pleasure, multiple orgasms will become easier and more enjoyable.

♀ Exercise ♂
Solo Ejaculation Awareness

This first exercise is similar to the peaking exercises, except there is a different emphasis at the point of ejaculation.

Set aside plenty of time for this exercise, and eliminate any potential distractions. Use deep breathing to relax yourself and get centered. When you are comfortable and relaxed, turn your focus to self-pleasuring. You are going to take yourself to a high level or arousal, peaking along the way by using your PC muscle. Be patient with yourself.

The Exercise Start by stroking your penis, using plenty of lubrication and the strokes you like best. Remember to keep breathing! Some men have a tendency to hold their breath when they start getting aroused.

Build your arousal to a level 6, then tense your PC muscle to peak. Keep stimulating yourself while you do the PC squeeze.

Let your arousal build to the higher levels, using your PC to control it. You've done this before, so you should be able to relax, focus, and enjoy. Peak several times, and when you get to your highest arousal level, be very aware of your body so you can experience your ejaculation differently, more focused than usual. You will be feeling for emission and expulsion, the different stages of ejaculation.

When you reach the point where you're going to come no matter what, stop stroking, open your eyes, and focus all your attention on your genitals. Breathe deeply and allow yourself to ejaculate. Don't do anything; just let it happen to you. See if you can feel the semen collecting in the base of your penis. Feel your PC muscle as it begins to spasm. Try to feel the semen moving up through your penis.

By stopping your stroke at the right time, you can make your ejaculation seem to last longer than it actually does. By being aware of the nuances of the process, you experience something of a time warp. You should be able to see that even when you've reached the point of no return, there is still time to stop the expulsion of semen if you want to.

The next set of exercises will explain how to use your PC to do just that.

♀ Exercise ♂
Ejaculation Awareness with Your Partner

Before beginning this exercise, pleasure your partner with a sensual massage or arousing caresses. You both should be relaxed and alert and have uninterrupted privacy.

The Exercise Lie on your back and have your partner caress your genitals. As she strokes and caresses you, peak several times around levels 5 and 6. Give your partner feedback, so she can back off and then intensify her caresses as you peak. After taking your arousal through several peaks, have your partner lie on her back, legs bent and spread, as you place yourself between them.

Stop for a moment, take a deep breath, and relax. Insert your penis and start slow, comfortable thrusting. Feel your movements and those of your partner. Peak again, taking yourself to higher levels. Use your PC muscle to maintain and control your arousal. When you reach the point of inevitability, both you and your partner stop moving—completely.

Open your eyes, breathe deeply, stay still, and focus. Try to feel the semen collecting in the base of your penis. Feel your PC muscle spasm. Notice the erupting sensation as the semen pushes up through your penis.

Most men keep thrusting during their orgasm while having intercourse, so stopping and letting go to concentrate on sensations during ejaculation is something new. Did it seem like your ejaculation lasted several seconds longer than it actually did? You might be surprised by the feelings you experience. It's not uncommon to feel spacey or out of body. Many men describe the feeling as an altered state of consciousness.

Practice this and the Solo Ejaculation Awareness exercise several times until you are confident in your awareness of the emission and expulsion phases of your ejaculation. When you are familiar and confident with them, you are now ready to advance to the next exercises—and the multiple orgasms they will bring!

♀ Exercise ♂
Solo Multiple Orgasm

In this exercise, you bring all the things you know about your body together with your sexual skills and control to build your pleasure, experience orgasm without release, then experience it again with release.

Before you begin this exercise, secure your privacy, take some deep breaths, and center yourself. Be alert but relaxed.

The Exercise Lie on your back or sit in a comfortable chair and begin a sensate focus genital caress. Build your arousal by peaking a few times at lower levels such as 4, 5, and 6.

After several low-level peaks, take yourself up much higher. Instead of using the slow, sensate focus–style of caressing, now start stroking your penis fast and intensely to get your arousal up to level 8.

When you reach level 8, tighten your PC muscle as hard as you can, take a very deep breath, and open your eyes. Slow your stroking down and let your arousal drop a little.

Now start stroking fast and hard again, aiming for a peak just over level 8. When you get there, again tense your PC really hard, open your eyes again, and take a very deep breath.

Slow your stroke down again, keep breathing slowly, and let your arousal subside. Repeat this process of quick-stroking to peak at levels 9 and just over 9. Then, stroke intensely up to your point of inevitability (9.9).

When you reach this point, slow down your stroke and squeeze your PC muscle according to your preferred method. Open your eyes and breathe deeply. Keep up the stroking as you squeeze. You now might feel the sensation of impending orgasm, but without an ejaculation if your PC squeezing was sufficient and at the right time. You will notice that although you had an orgasm, you still have your erection and feel ready for more arousal. If it didn't work in this instance, practice again at another time. There are several things to coordinate, and it requires fine-tuning. When you finally get it, you will never forget it. It's like learning to ride the proverbial bicycle.

Now let your orgasm subside, and take a breather. Let your arousal drop down a couple levels and breathe deeply. Stroke your penis lightly, to maintain your erection. Stay slow and mellow for a little while.

When you are ready to pick up the pace again, stroke fast and hard to bring yourself to arousal level 9 and beyond. Keep stroking all the way over the edge this time. Don't try to stop. Don't tighten your PC. Let yourself blow into a full orgasm with ejaculation.

That's it—you are now a multiorgasmic man! Repeat the above exercise several times to lock in the rhythm and technique that works for you before moving to the next step. Be patient and take your time.

♀ Exercise ♂
Multiple Orgasm with Your Partner

This exercise takes some time and can't be rushed, so make sure you have at least an hour of quiet, uninterrupted time, preferably more. You will do peaking while having intercourse, but in a very different way than in previous exercises, using rapid, vigorous thrusting without spending a lot of time between peaks. This exercise is very intense and requires energy and concentration. It is crucial that your partner stop moving every time you do.

The Exercise Start by pleasuring your partner, then lie back comfortably while she begins caressing you in a sensual manner. As your partner works her way to your genitals, stay relaxed, focusing on the pleasurable sensations and your rising arousal. Let her caress for her own pleasure, with her fingers, palms, mouth, or lips.

When your arousal builds, do your first peak around level 4, and squeeze your PC muscle to bring your arousal down. Peak again at level 5, drop down, peak at level 6, and then drop down again.

Now, switch positions with your partner. Have her lie on her back with her legs raised and knees bent. Rest back on your knees and thighs, between your partner's legs.

Insert your penis and begin gentle thrusting, then pick up the pace quickly. Thrust deep and hard until your arousal reaches level 8.

Slow down your thrusting a bit and do your PC muscle squeeze. Your partner should stop moving, also. Open your eyes and take a deep breath. Allow your arousal to drop down a little.

Begin again with easy, relaxed thrusting. Get your energy level up and start thrusting harder and faster. When you reach just past level 8, thrust more slowly and do your PC squeezes. Again, open your eyes and take a good deep breath. Let your arousal subside.

Get ready to go at it again. Thrusting hard and fast, climb to level 9. When you feel orgasm is close, slow down and squeeze. Open your eyes and take a deep breath. Back your arousal down one level.

Wait a moment, then continue. Thrust past level 9 and do the slower-squeeze-breathe routine. At the high levels, you may notice you need to squeeze harder and breathe deeper to keep control. It is important for your partner to stop moving just as soon as you do.

Now for the finale! After you momentarily drop back from that highest peak, get going one more time, all the way to the point of inevitability. Your target is that point between emission and expulsion. As your reach it, stay focused, tuned into the strength of your sexual power. Time will seem to stretch out at this point.

When you hit that point of 9.9, slow, squeeze, breathe, and open your eyes. You may now experience your first nonejaculatory orgasm during intercourse! You can do this again or move on to an ejaculatory orgasm. Of course, you may simply choose to stop; there is no law that says you must ejaculate during intercourse.

Come down by resting with some slow, gentle thrusting. Slow thrusting will help you maintain your erection. Don't worry if your erection loses some stiffness. It will come back soon.

After a brief rest, speed up the intensity of your movements. This time, let your arousal plunge ahead—don't stop it, just thrill in the deepness and power it now has. Let it drive you all the way over the edge into another orgasm, complete with a forceful ejaculation.

Can you see how lovemaking like this leads to simultaneous orgasms later? With all the thrusting and stopping, it is likely your partner was peaking too and drawing nearer and nearer to her own orgasm.

All these exercises sound pretty great, don't they? You may find, however, that they are easier to read about than to do—in the beginning. At first, you might have a "partial" orgasm or feel like you missed it altogether. Perhaps during the first orgasm, you had a partial ejaculation. Or, after having one orgasm, you found it difficult to reach another one. Don't despair. Anything worth having is worth working for, right? Virtually anyone who uses these methods and really wants to, can have multiple orgasms. Some men get the hang of it right away, but for most it takes much practice and *patience*.

Multiple orgasms also take some experimentation and adaptation of techniques to suit your individual style. You may find you need or would like to make some adjustments for yourself. For example, one long, hard PC squeeze or several mild squeezes may work better for you. Also, the timing of your squeeze in relation to your thrusting can make a difference. Some men prefer it on the in-stroke, others prefer the out-stroke, and others just before reversing direction, whether it be deep at the cervix, the vaginal opening, or someplace in between.

However you do it, just be sure to keep a positive attitude and have fun. Remember, this is all about enhancing something you already enjoy! Here's another encouraging note: once you've succeeded, it does become easier—automatic, say some. Your body becomes conditioned to responding in this new activity. "Muscle memory" helps it learn the routine. And when it becomes easier to achieve with less effort, the pleasure can be incredible, nothing less than profound. Our friend *Max* described the sensations he experiences during nonejaculatory orgasms like this: "It feels electrical. Like a bolt of steely-cool electricity running through my body."

Post-Coital Pleasures

Sharing the process of learning how to have multiple orgasms is an intimate endeavor. Experiencing your own and your lover's multiple orgasms can be deeply meaningful, in ways you would never expect. How do you two find it? Are you ready to go to sleep afterwards, or do you want to conquer the world? Do you want to wrap yourself around your partner, or are you too satiated for more touch? People's reactions can differ widely from each other and even from their previous orgasmic experiences. You may feel in sync with each other or feel quite separate. Both reactions are normal.

If you or your partner find any of these activities disturbing in any way, give thoughtful consideration to why. Is there something going on internally that you need to be more aware of? Are there hidden prohibitions about feeling so much pleasure? Are you unable to let go completely or to let go with your lover? Don't pressure yourself or your partner to go further with the exercises until you have resolved the things that make you uncomfortable.

If you find that you are pushing yourself to perform, forget it. Your body is a magnificent machine. It has an incredible memory, especially when it really likes something. Trust yourself to get there—wherever there is—when you are ready and willing.

Meanwhile, even if you aren't doing everything perfectly the first time (after all, who does?) you can be a great support for each other. An encouraging hug and kiss go a long way toward helping each of you get over nervousness or performance pressure. Tell each other how patient you are willing to be. You can't repeat too often how special these experiences are for your relationship or how much you love each other. You may feel vulnerable at these times. It is reassuring to know that your partner holds your feelings in the highest regard. This is a life-long process. Don't forget to have fun.

Part Three
Enhancing the Bond

Chapter 8
And Now, the Moment You've All Been Waiting For

Lord Illingworth: The Book of Life begins with a man and a woman in a garden.
Mrs. Allonby: It ends with Revelations.

—Oscar Wilde, *A Woman of No Importance*

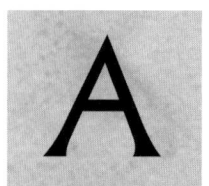

All of the preparation is done. All your mindset, physical readiness, and emotional determination is practiced and in place. It will now all come together. And with ease. Sure, it is going to take some fine-tuning, good humor, and desire, but it will happen. Why? Because you have earned the right to have it happen. You have also progressed far enough to use our suggestions on how to ignite the experience of simultaneous orgasm as a catalyst for your own creativity and uniqueness.

So, you may ask, how is it possible that this chapter, the one that finally tells us how to achieve simultaneous orgasm, can be shorter than all of those before it? It is possible because, at this point, you only need to aim and fire.

If you have followed the program to this point and worked through the exercises, take a moment to feel really good about yourself. Reflect on the changes you've experienced since you began this process. If you didn't really believe it was possible to make your sex life better and better, we bet you're convinced now! Have you noticed what a difference the PC exercises make? If you are no longer doing them daily, get back on track. Then pay close attention to how much your sensations deepen when you are making love. Just enjoying these pleasurable effects may help you remember to include them in your daily routine.

Notice also what has happened to your confidence levels and your eagerness to make time for intimacy with your partner. A lot of good can come from completing the solo and partner exercises in the preceding chapters. If you feel your foundation skills still need work, there's no need to rush here. Take whatever time you need, repeating the solo and partner exercises of previous chapters until you are sexually and intimately satisfied and are ready to move on to the next area. The whole point of this program is to give you the skills—physical, sensual, emotional, and mental—to bring about the exquisite ecstasy that sexual union has to offer. But *you* invoke them as and when they suit you and your relationship.

The Fine Art of Hovering and Triggering

When you both are confident of your ability to modulate your arousal, last as long as you like during intercourse, and reach orgasm with intercourse, you are ready to learn the final skills of sexual finesse that will put simultaneous orgasm in reach whenever you want it. These skills don't have technical names, but we call them "hovering" and "triggering." For all practical purposes, hovering is equivalent to a concept you know and have already practiced, namely plateauing.

To experience deliberate simultaneous orgasms you need to know how to hover at dizzying heights of arousal until you're both ready to come, and how to trigger the irrevocable explosion of orgasm for your partner or yourself. When we speak of hovering, we refer to the ability to maintain that intense arousal of being on the verge. If you are going to reach orgasm together, you both have to be at or around that delicate edge. Also, hovering will enable you to prolong the pleasures of your lovemaking when you both wish to do that. Another time hovering comes in handy is when one of you hits the heights before the other and wants to wait on the verge while the other catches up. Generally, we find that women are able to hover at high levels of arousal more easily than men.

Triggering is when the flame of arousal hits the dynamite of orgasm. When you reach the point in your lovemaking where one partner is ready to come, and you both know you'd like to reach orgasm together, you can do one of two things: The partner who is closest to climax can trigger the other, or the partner who is not quite there can use an internal trigger to set off his or her own orgasm. Don't feel intimidated by the concept of a trigger—what we're talking about are the little things you already do (or say) to take yourself or each other over the edge. The more you know about what turns your partner on as well as what it takes to get fully aroused yourself, the more help you can be to each other.

Riding the Heights of Pleasure

Hovering and triggering can feel a lot like riding a roller coaster. Remember what that's like? You begin by cruising along, taking in the scenery and tasting the joy of the ride. Then a few quick dips here and there get your attention and create anticipation for what's ahead. You gain momentum, riding through wild ups and downs, and then you are thrown into intense awareness of the sensations in your body. As the feelings intensify, you find yourself swooping and soaring through breathtaking twists and turns and maybe even a loop-de-loop! You hold on for dear life, and you feel yourself on the brink of completely dissolving—or spinning off into space. The thrills are dizzying. How much more can you take?

Then, in a blaze of sensations, climax approaches. Time slows; you are completely aware of your internal sensations and of your beloved as well. You could choose to hold fast and make the last dizzying ascent alone. Instead, you grab hold of each other. Together, as one, you're thrown through the vortex of orgasm in a great burst of sound, sensation, and energy. With release, things slow, bringing contentment, exhaustion, and sweet peace.

If you recall the peaking, plateauing, and multiple orgasm exercises, a lot of this should be familiar. Now you are ready to play around with your lovemaking, to introduce the possibility of stepping over the edge into the abyss of ecstasy together. When you do this, you'll find the pleasure doesn't just double—it increases exponentially! This is where all your practice and fine-tuning will come together.

Does the idea seem somewhat intimidating to one or both of you? Before going for the gusto, we recommend that couples make a date for a dress rehearsal. Dress rehearsals are relaxed opportunities to bring all your talents to the stage without the pressure of having to perform perfectly. They strengthen your positive attitude and give you the sense of accomplishment that comes with success, so that your goal becomes easier to attain. Another example of this can be found in therapy, where therapists boost self-confidence in people by having them imagine how a confident person would feel and act, and then role-play being confident. By acting confident they learn how to *be* confident, and true confidence soon takes root. Because of the complex mind-body dynamic, dress rehearsals have the power to bring about real internal change. Studies have shown that people who smile and pretend to be happy soon start feeling genuinely happy.

Admittedly, behavioral and emotional changes require more than simply acting in a prescribed way. You need to believe in and internalize what you want. Yet the fact remains that going through the motions of a desired behavior helps improve your chances for success.

So the next step in coming together is to simulate the experience of having simultaneous orgasms. Don't think of this as faking it. In your dress rehearsal, you will draw on all the skills you've learned up to this point, to show your brain and body exactly what you want.

♀ Exercise ♂
The Dress Rehearsal

For your dress rehearsal, make a date and set the stage. Approach this not as an exercise but as a "night in the life" of the two of you. Begin with your usual introductions: undressing each other or undressing for each other; rubbing each other's backs, necks, or feet; taking a sensuous shower; kissing and cuddling.

The Exercise Begin your lovemaking practice by hovering, first alone and then together. You can do this by pleasuring yourself or each other as you did in the previous peaking and plateauing exercises (Chapters 5 and 6).

Focus loving attention on your genitals, building your desire and savoring the levels of your arousal as it increases. Give each other feedback and direction when necessary. You want to climb to a very high level of arousal, hovering at the edge of orgasm.

To hover at a particular level, close enough to climax yet far enough to maintain control, experiment a bit. Here are things you can try that we have found helpful:

- Change the stimulation slightly from your usual touch—a little more slowly or softly, perhaps. For example, stroking her clitoris slightly off-center might keep a woman's arousal at its height without increasing it.

- Remember to breathe, and breathe deeply.

- Focus on your sensations. Savor what you're feeling. Let each sensation be the intense, attention-riveting experience it should be. Enjoy the variety of pleasures you feel.

- Let go and stay relaxed. This is play, not work! You can be very aroused and still be relaxed. Concentrate, but have fun.

Next, see if you can hover during intercourse. Fall into your favorite position, and begin moving slowly and sensuously. Move in sync as you speed up or slow down and fall into your natural rhythm together. Couples with well-established intimate relationships often find this happens almost automatically. If this wasn't common for you before, you may find it happening more naturally as you develop deeper sexual awareness through this program. As two lovers become familiar with one another, their body rhythms begin to mesh and they learn each other's styles. This is one of the great rewards of an enduring, deeply-bonded relationship.

Allow yourself to relax into a deep pleasure state and, with your touch, encourage your partner to do the same. Trust nature to take its course, without trying to make anything happen. Feel confident that the learning you've done so far will carry you all the way through.

As you reach the higher levels of arousal together, one of you may come much closer to orgasm than the other. That's fine. It is not necessary to wait for the other to catch up. Whoever reaches the brink first, go for it. Let the orgasm rock your body. Let the energy run through you to your partner. Open up to it—and to your partner.

If you are not the first one to reach orgasm, vividly experience your lover's orgasm as your own. Move your body orgasmically. Feel your heart pound, your muscles spasm, your lungs pant. Experience the energy of your partner's climax coursing through you, and let it connect you. If you normally get vocal when you come, make the same noises. Don't be surprised if this actually sends you into your own climax. It is not uncommon for the simulation to turn into the real thing.

Let your coming together experience move beyond physical reactions. Be aware of your emotions. Hold a vivid mental image of yourself experiencing a deep and satisfying orgasm. Be aware of your loving bond together and the dynamics that drive your attraction to each other. Open your mind to really get into it, but don't do it in a way that puts walls between you, such as fantasizing. Instead, be very present in the moment, allowing yourself to become vulnerable and open. Melt into each other, feeling a sense of connection that touches your very essence.

When it is over, reflect on how coming together magnifies the intensity of your ecstatic release. Does it overtake you? Elevate you? Overwhelm you? What you have had is the most exalted, generous kind of sharing.

After the Dress Rehearsal: Opening Night

How did the dress rehearsal go? Are you ready for the real thing, or are you happy practicing a bit more? Have you experienced a true coming together yet? After one or more dress rehearsals, you might want to try some techniques that will take you even closer to having a simultaneous orgasm at will. During intercourse, when one of you reaches the hovering heights of arousal, you can help the other catch up.

For her pleasure:

- Try adding clitoral stimulation or increasing the angle of penetration. The High Rider position (described in Chapter 6), in which the man leans forward over his partner, putting pressure on her clitoris with his pubic bone, does both these things very nicely.

- Thrust deeply, hitting the G-spot, to step up her full-body arousal and move her closer to climax.

- Add anything erotic: kissing, nibbling, licking. Women tend to be especially responsive to verbal cues. Some say the sound of their partner's voice during lovemaking is a major turn-on.

- Share your arousal. Talk sexy and use sound to communicate your excitement. Thrill your partner by letting her know she's very desirable to you and has taken you to the heights of arousal.

For his pleasure:

- Let yourself go. Murmuring encouragement, slapping or grabbing your partner's back or buttocks, and pulling him into you can add to his excitement.

- Encourage him to watch. Men tend to be very responsive to visual stimulation. Let him see how he penetrates you. Free your expressions and your body to communicate your pleasure.

- Help him focus on the sounds and smells of lovemaking. This can really enhance your arousal as well as his.

For both of you, if your partner is ready to come but you are still getting aroused, try switching to a different position, changing the angle of penetration, or changing the speed or pressure. This will work as long as you can keep thrusting and bringing yourself closer to climax.

There are many, many ways partners learn to hover and play with each other—as many ways as there are couples. Communication, both verbal and nonverbal, is the key. You must both communicate clearly and listen attentively and patiently.

• • •

We wish we could say that after one or two (or five, or ten) hovering sessions like these, one big exercise will bring you to a breathtaking climax together—now and forever. But the truth is that simultaneous orgasm will come to you in the ways that are unique to you and your lovemaking as a couple. By learning to hover for as long you like, you can take yourselves to a place where you can trigger simultaneous orgasms whenever you wish to share them. Orgasmic triggers are lovemaking secrets you *already* know—you just have to rediscover them as such.

Pull That Trigger!

A trigger is just what it sounds like—the final action that sends you over the edge. You probably already know several things that do it for you and your partner: tugging on his earlobe with your teeth . . . groaning with pleasure in her ear. We all have our own cues. Partners who are well acquainted with each other's sexuality often know just what to do, and when, to help their lovers climax. These usually aren't things you learn on a first or second date. Rather, they are the gems you're blessed with as gifts of intimate sharing. We think that one of the supreme joys of an intimate relationship is to discover your lover's personal cues, the marks of his or her deep arousal.

Triggers take many forms and can involve any of the senses. Sometimes, partners have similar or even identical triggers. Each person may have several favorite triggers, allowing for variety and surprise in a couple's repertoire. Some people can come "on demand"—all it takes is for their partners to tell them to come, in just the right tone of voice, and *voilà!* Some partners are so tuned in to each other that when one starts to orgasm, it's enough to trigger orgasm in the other.

Discovering each other's orgasmic triggers takes time, experimentation, and communication. It also requires vulnerability. Sharing at such a profound level of intimacy creates a powerful bond, and it is this bond that makes coming together so exquisite. Allowing your orgasm to be triggered by your partner involves surrender, an offering of your self without reserve. This is part of the experience of "assertive submission." It can feel magical, and it should—something wondrous is happening to you.

Hi Ho Trigger, Awaaay!

Following are some examples of simultaneous orgasm "triggers" generously offered by clients and friends.

I get flooded with sexual energy, waiting to explode. When his pace starts to quicken, I grind down with my hips, bringing him in deeper. This sets us both off.

—Jamie, 27

We were newlyweds when I discovered that a single, well-timed nibble on her neck or shoulder would bring her into orgasm. It still works today!

—Miles, 58

When I know she is about to come, I sometimes think about how happy I am going to be ejaculating inside her while she spasms. That makes me come in about three seconds.

—Robert, 28

As we have changed, so have our sexual triggers. Right now, I like to get on top, pin his hands down, and let him know that orgasm's right around the corner. He surrenders willfully.

—April, 35

Sometimes I think I can feel his penis swell up just before he orgasms. When I am already very aroused, like a 9+, and that happens, I think to myself, 'He is really hot and in love with me,' which triggers my own orgasm.

—Sandra, 22

I wrap myself around her, as closely as I can, and breathe in her ear. As she moves against me, our bodies and breathing seem to join together. Our orgasm comes as one giant wave.

—Bob, 40

> *There is this very sensitive spot, right on the ridge of my penis. When she is going to come, by thrusting in a particular way I create just a little more stimulation right there, which makes me come every time.*
>
> —Philip, 32

> *When she starts to scream "Oh my God! I'm coming! I am coming!" while I am at a high level of arousal, it immediately kick-starts me into an orgasm of my own.*
>
> —Max, 43

> *I can raise my hips and press my pelvic area hard up against him as he is coming. The stimulation of his thrusting and my extra pelvic pressure kicks it off every time.*
>
> —Julie, 34

> *Whenever Hank is about to orgasm, he puts his hands under my butt, pulling our pelvis swellings tight against each other, and hisses in my ear, "Come my beauty; come with me." It works every time.*
>
> —Annie, 41

Coming Together— Again and Again and Again

The French expression for orgasm literally means "little death." At the moment of sexual climax what dies, if only momentarily, is our sense of separateness. In climax, two become as one. This is truer of simultaneous orgasm than of any other sexual act. Poets write of two souls flowing into each other. The artist, Alexander Grey, depicts the moment of orgasm as auras blazing into color, blending and merging as one. Lovers speak of shifting into an altered state of consciousness or feeling electrified by the sexual energy currents.

Our friend *Shondra* described her experiences of simultaneous orgasm this way: "When you come it's such a release of energy, and when you do it together—Boom!—it's so intense, you can feel it in your eyeballs. . . .

I notice that when we aren't using rubbers or diaphragms, I can actually feel the electricity in my vaginal area. It's just amazingly different."

Her lover, *Keith*, adds, "Physically, mentally, it creates a much more elaborate kind of joining. There's this very special atmosphere."

Your learning curve doesn't have to stop with your first intentional simultaneous orgasm. Consider it the beginning of a whole new phase of extraordinary lovemaking. The ways and means to bring about simultaneous orgasms are limited only by your imagination and desires.

Where can you go from here? Well, that's up to you. We would like to suggest some enjoyable options.

> **Mutual masturbation:** If you find it thrilling to watch each other, or if the thought of your partner masturbating arouses you, it can be very exciting to see if you can pleasure yourself and still stay aware enough of your partner to climax at the same time. Couples who enjoy this often find that the woman needs more stimulation than the man, so her lover might hold her first, caressing her breasts or kissing her belly as she begins. Then when she gets close, he takes himself in hand.
>
> **Mutual pleasuring:** You can also pleasure each other by escalating your petting until you come together. Try starting a session like this by mixing a special massage oil and stroking it on each other's bodies, as if you were oiling up for a sexual Olympics. Caressing each other's full bodies can be highly arousing and satisfying, because it feeds the whole body's hunger for touch instead of just concentrating on the genitals. As you pleasure each other, free yourself to make sounds—communicate your excitement. Try to bring your breathing into sync as you come closer and closer to the heights of arousal and the brink of orgasm. Then, take each other in hand, and push each other over the edge.
>
> **Sexy 69:** If you enjoy the 69 position, experiment with oral simultaneous orgasms. Get into a tangle of arms and legs and savor all the complex sensations you are giving and receiving. This may be a bit more challenging, because it can be difficult to concentrate on your

own pleasure when you are also giving pleasure in this way. You might want to try it with the lights off the first time, to limit visual distractions. Mutual oral sex can also be a highly arousing and demanding position. If it works for you, go for it. If it doesn't, savor this position for its own merits, then try something else.

Anal pleasuring: Simultaneous orgasm is also possible with anal intercourse if that is something you and your lover enjoy. The same principals of arousal apply. Women can receive lots of different types of stimulation at once, and some men find the tighter opening highly arousing. Since this is also challenging, you might want to save it for when you're both feeling energetic and confident about your ability to modulate your arousal.

You can also mix and match positions and techniques in the same extended lovemaking session. Be careful about proper hygiene when including anal sex in your lovemaking, or you might introduce bacteria into the urethra or vagina and cause infection.

Playing with Mood and Style

We've talked mostly about technique and attitude in the last couple of chapters. The real joy comes in using them to express your own, personal style. Of course, your moods and interests might vary: tender and romantic one night, voyeuristic the next, and slightly dangerous and devil-may-care another night. As far as we're concerned, everything you do and feel is all right unless it involves hurting or coercing your partner.

To stoke your imagination, here is a list of sexual styles with settings and props that can help cultivate the mood. Women, remember that men are visually oriented, so consider your attire when setting the scene. Men, don't forget that women have a keener sense of smell and are often turned on by all their senses.

Adolescent: Go for a spin and park at Lovers' Point, or check out the space beneath the bleachers at your high school on a sultry summer night. If you can swing it, rent a car that was popular the year the two of you met. Get copies of the music you listened to as teens and the kind of liquor you once sneaked from your parents' liquor cabinet (but go easy on the drinking—you want to experience each other and not the liquor, and you don't want to drink and drive). Or try setting yourselves up with the things teens find hot today, and giggle and laugh your way through a "raving" sexual encounter of "infectious grooves."

Au Natural: If the weather's agreeable, get out into nature. Spend a few days in the desert, in the woods, or at a private beach. Make love with abandon in the fresh air, feeling the warm leaves (or sand, or rocks) against your bodies. Find a secluded field along the road during an autumn drive. Get in touch with the natural force of your sexuality.

Animal: If the temperatures are too cold outside, gather up animal print sheets, fur rugs, and musk incense. Install a small running fountain in your living room or bedroom. Gather up feathers that tickle, and trail them over each other's body.

Athletic: Book a room at a ski chalet, or reproduce the look in a corner of your home. Make love on the deck of a boat. After a weight-training session at the local gym (or a run, or strenuous bicycle ride), strip off your clothes and finish your workout with each other. Come up with creative ways to use the Universal machine or a weight bench in your own home. Scent your lovemaking room with something clean-smelling, like wintergreen or the eucalyptus used in sports ointments. Get into the sexiest spandex attire you can find.

Bawdy: Go to a Renaissance Fair together, dress in costume, and feed each other the juiciest fruits and meats you can find. Eat with your fingers. Read each other Chaucer's bawdier poems over ale—or read Erica Jong over cheap wine. Meet up at a local pub, then book yourself a room above it to retire to.

Cultured: Get your room ready beforehand, so when you return from the opera or ballet you'll return to a love nest with ambient lighting, fine wines, savory delicacies, and artful floral arrangements. Consider keeping the pearls, high heels, or necktie on for a bit longer than usual. If you're fluent in another language, make an agreement to speak to each other only in French, say, or Russian.

Domineering: Go for urban chic. Add chrome or leather accents to your wardrobe and private sex room. Shop for a black or red bustier, restraining straps, and other toys together. Try out dominant and submissive roles—with full consent, of course.

Dramatic: If you've got a theatrical bent, concoct any number of scenarios: You could meet as your favorite famous lovers in history or on television, or play archetypes, such as spy/counterspy, biker/farm girl, goddess/consort. Meet in public places, or make private dates. Have a secret rendezvous at a romantic inn, or greet each other at the airport as if long-separated lovers.

Erotic: Shop for great nudes or Indian or Oriental depictions of couples, and decorate your bedroom. Think texture and sensation, and gather the right props and music to match. Feed each other oysters or other aphrodisiacs. Use chocolate sauce, whipping cream, sex creams, or ice cubes to tantalize. (We'll never forget the sex scene in the movie, *The Other Side of Midnight,* in which a woman very skilled in the art of lovemaking used a menthol cream on her lover to drive him wild.)

Ethereal: Dress yourselves and your surroundings in flowing white. Invest in a few Tibetan bowls. Light jasmine- or frangipani-scented incense. Spend time in meditation or doing chakra breathing, or chant together to bring yourselves in tune before lovemaking. Imagine making love to the Shiva and Shakti energy in each other.

Kinky: Have phone sex that turns into real sex. Share your favorite fantasy or look to erotic magazines to find one that really turns you both on. Work out the details you will need to set the mood. You're on your own here, because only you know what you fantasize about.

Nurturing: Set out the futon and the special massage pillows, and take turns massaging each other. Or turn on the Jacuzzi or sit for a while in the hot tub. Scent the room with aromatherapy oils. Let your lovemaking be languorous, slow, and sweet. Brew up soothing herbal tea for when you're done.

Playful: Go shopping for toys together. Puppets are always fun, and sometimes it's easier to ask for outrageous things when you're speaking in a high, squeaky voice. Stay up late and play strip poker or naked Twister. Blow bubbles on each other's naked bodies.

Romantic: Court each other as you did (or didn't do!) in your early courtship days. Take your romance to new heights by trying the Karezza method used in the famed Oneida community (*karezza* means "caress" in Italian). It calls for a great deal of caressing and kissing and a steady stream of love talk. The objective is for the man to "pour out his soul in as poetic an expression of his love as he can, letting it pour out like a slow-moving river," according to Bernard Jensen, who describes the method in his book, *Love, Sex and Nutrition* (Garden City, NY: Avery Publishing Group, 1988).

Unbridled: Ravish each other in the woodshed, or duck behind the rose bushes. Start something at the kitchen sink or in the laundry room. Have a secluded picnic in the park. Explore each other in the back row of the local X-rated movie house. Bring your unbridled sexuality into the ordinary—or extraordinary—happenings of your daily life.

This list could go on and on, but these suggestions should get you started. If it has been a long time since you've let your mind wander down these fanciful tracks, check out some erotic literature to see what catches your interest. You might be surprised to find that your tastes have changed over the years and that new turn-ons are tempting you to try them.

The Multiple Simultaneous Orgasm

At some point, you'll feel confident enough of all of your new skills—peaking and plateauing, mutual orgasm, hovering and triggering—to bring them together in one big, continual bang. This is easier than you might imagine. Once you know how to have a multiple orgasm and how to hover and trigger, you can do this.

When you attempt this, make sure you are feeling energetic and clearheaded, and make sure you have a generous amount of time. Be prepared to surrender to a long lovemaking session and the satiation that will follow. This isn't something you're going to want to attempt on a Friday night after a particularly hectic and trying week at work, but you may want to plan it for a weekend after you've wrapped up the big project and gone for a rejuvenating massage.

♀ Exercise ♂
Making the Multiple Simultaneous Orgasm

There is no straightforward path to multiple simultaneous orgasms, no secret recipe, exercise, or dance step. This section is an exercise in improvisation, synthesizing all that you have learned with your own life experience and creativity. This improvisation is guided by the ebb and flow of your mutual sexual energies. You must throw yourselves into the waters of arousal and desire and draw on your sexual skills to ride the rapids of arousal, orgasm, arousal, and more orgasm.

Savor your lovemaking with the indulgence, attention, and devotion that you'd bring to a seven-course feast. Pace yourselves and build your momentum slowly over time, knowing you're going to be doing this for a while. The mindset is very different than when you're both building up to the "big one" together. With multiple simultaneous orgasm, you create your arousal through a sequence of increasing arousal, hovering, orgasm, and perhaps triggering and more waves or a cascade of orgasm.

Speaking of cascades, you women aren't going to want a gusher-style orgasm first, because after the gusher you are likely going to feel so sated that you will want to stop. For some women, multiple orgasms occur most easily when there has been a whole night of loving and foreplay beforehand, so you men might want to pace yourself. Just get yourself into a space where you joyfully follow your sensations, and allow the inspiration for what comes next to arise in the moment. Forget about having a goal, and see what you can do to heighten the process.

Throughout your lovemaking remember to keep breathing, releasing any surface tensions, and focus on your sensations and your lover. Practice shifting your focus throughout the long hours of lovemaking so that each of your senses is filled to the brim. Then, when you've both had enough, let your pleasure bubble over the top, sending you into the flood of release again and again and again!

Luxuriating in the Post-Coital Embrace

Just as it is important to have a generous amount of uninterrupted time for lovemaking, it is important to share some "let down" time afterward. Give yourself time to enjoy your newfound feelings of closeness before you shift your attention to something else. The experience of simultaneous orgasm, especially multiple simultaneous orgasm, is very profound. You need to ground yourselves after sharing that kind of energy and vulnerability. Embrace, kiss, caress, whisper whatever inspires you. Or simply curl up and breathe deeply together. One couple we know lies together, touching only their fingertips and gazing into each other's eyes, until their energies subside. Allow yourselves to enjoy that wholly relaxed feeling as long as you can.

Since a long, extended lovemaking session can take a lot of energy and focus, you should also take care to replenish yourselves afterwards. Asian lovers (especially those in India) often prepare special foods before lovemaking that will help revive them afterward. These are usually milk- or protein-based. Other couples find that a juicy sweet, such as fresh tangerines or chilled grapes, are most refreshing. Sparkling waters are a wonderful way to refresh your insides and cool down your outsides.

If your lovemaking session has lasted into the evening, consider ordering dinner in. Or if you want to feel like kids again, share popsicles, cookies, or other goodies on the sofa while you relax in front of a good movie. If you can, take a stroll in the evening, hand in hand, wholly relaxed, your senses keen from a whole day of enjoying each other. Relax in a warm bath and wash every inch of each other lovingly. Whatever you decide to do, let the echoes of the union you just created enrich you and imbue your private time with meaning.

Chapter 9
Don't Make Lust Last, Make It First!

Couples who have grown to love and trust each other over the years form an unparalleled support system. Their shared history, steadfast commitment, and appreciation of each other create a reservoir of peace and contentment. It's a comfort so deep you rarely hear people talking about it.

—Dr. Patricia Love and Jo Robinson, *Hot Monogamy*

ovelty is exciting. It makes the brain (and perhaps other parts as well) sit up and pay attention. And that's what it takes to keep a marriage or long-term relationship exciting. Fortunately, none of us are born one-dimensional beings, but our relationships can become that way.

What is so exciting for new lovers is the exploration, the "getting to know you" part of the relationship. The heart wonders: In what way is this person like me? What interests, values, or goals do we have in common? In what ways can we share joy together? In what ways are we different? How will our life together draw me beyond the small sphere I call myself and into a life that's larger and roomier where the rest of me can emerge? Will I be able to tolerate this process? Will the other person? Can he (she) hang in there with me? What will I bring to my partner?

In relationships that stay ever new, couples never stop asking these questions. They reveal and share, perhaps finding themselves in a loving tug of war as the impulse for growth ripples through their relationships. Sure, they may make regular retreats into the safety zone of "how we've always done it," but they also cultivate an openness to the interests and opportunities that the other brings.

If the woman wakes up one morning with the desire to make exotic masks fashioned after ones she has dreamed about—and then wear them to bed—her partner might not only agree but offer to help her hunt down the materials she needs and find just the right world-beat music to match. If the man wakes up with the desire to have sex with an anonymous stranger in bicycle shorts and dark sunglasses, his partner laughingly consents and agrees to meet him in an out-of-town pub where they can act out the fantasy. The point is, they stay open enough to life and each other to say "Sure, I'm willing to try that," instead of "No, that's not me." They are courageous enough to keep revealing new parts of themselves and to be gently insistent on giving these parts expression within the relationship.

It is in this spirit that we present the following suggestions for intimate play. All of these ideas are time- and clinic-tested, and they have their own unique reason for being. That is why we suggest you try each one, at least once, at your own pace. Each is designed to draw out a different aspect of your sexual being, in a way that will bring new life into your intimate relationship.

Some of these "games" are just plain fun. Others cut a bit deeper into who you really are and leave you a bit more raw and exposed to each other. They will help strengthen the ties that bind you and develop a fuller respect and appreciation for your differences. Also, don't underestimate the power of a good shared laugh. Let go! Take a chance! Otherwise, you may face an even greater risk: boredom.

Granted, these little games will require you to set aside the time to do them, and by time we mean quality time. Don't try them at 11 p.m. after an exhausting day working or taking care of the kids. Make a date with each other, just like when you were younger, and don't break that date unless there is a real emergency. You have to tend to your relationship with each other if you want it to survive.

We'd like to make one more suggestion. Always start these love games with a moment or two of appreciation for each other and your love. Think about what you've been through together already and how you felt when your love was at its most intense. Think of the ways in which your partner has expressed love and acceptance in the past, and from that place of feeling accepted, let yourself go fully into the exercise. Remember, this is a good, loving person you see in front of you. Maybe this person is a bit difficult at times, or incomprehensible, or even seemingly at odds with you, but look closely and deeply. Your partner is there for you right now: trusting, ready, and desirous of only you.

A relationship that bonds two autonomous, self-respecting persons, who esteem and honor the differences their partner brings to the table, is a magnificent celebration of life.

Here you go.

Sexual Epoxy through Play

No one says intimacy has to be serious—have some fun! There are two versions of the following exercise: one is long (four to six hours), and one is short (thirty minutes to one hour). Choose the one that fits best with your needs and schedule, or you may want to find time for both.

♀ Exercise ♂
Ask for What You Want: Version 1

In this exercise, one of you plans a four- to six-hour date for the two of you. If you choose this version, plan to repeat the exercise, reversing roles, within the month. The purpose of the exercise is to allow the person planning the date to share something about who he or she is with the other. The activity should express that individual's unique style. For instance, if the person planning the date is a romantic, he or she might want to plan a weekend getaway at a romantic country inn. The planner should, however, choose an activity that both will like.

If you are the planner, it is your responsibility to handle all of the details: making the reservation, getting the baby-sitter, bringing the wine. The date may include sex, but it doesn't need to. If you are the other partner, you don't have to do anything at all, except pack accordingly. You should also bring enthusiasm to the activity. Show your appreciation for your partner's planning and thought. That's what makes this exercise work. If the activity is something that makes you uncomfortable, you always have the right to say no.

Following are a few examples of how four to six hours might be planned.

Romantic Style, Away from Home Find a hotel with dining and dancing and make a reservation for one night's stay. Call the hotel in advance and ask to have flowers and champagne (or any other favorite beverage) waiting in the room when you arrive. Ask your partner to pack an overnight bag with a few of his or her sexiest and most comfortable things, including something you especially like, and let your partner know the departure time. When you arrive at the hotel, go straight to your room and slip into something comfortable (perhaps silk lounging outfits you've picked up for the occasion?). Sip your champagne and take in your new surroundings. Then trade massages. Or make love. Rest, get dressed, and go out for dinner and dancing. Spend a good night together. In the morning, sleep in, make love, and order room service—not necessarily in that order.

Romantic Style, at Home Have your partner put on an outfit you love and invite him or her to a candlelight dinner at a set time. Cook (or purchase) a meal that can be prepared in advance so there's not much to do once you have begun eating. Play music you both enjoy and light candles for ambiance. You could even hire a musician (music students are often inexpensive) to serenade you during dinner! After dinner, sit by a fire and make out (remember the old days?). Undress each other and make love with abandon on the living room floor.

Erotic Date Order an erotic video from the Sexuality Library (see the *Resources* section of this book). Many of these films are more sensuous than hard-core. (Soft-core films tend to be more appealing to women.) Set a time to meet your partner, giving instructions on how to dress. You might even want to purchase the clothes you'd like your partner to wear. Choose something that you'll find erotic. Then watch your partner dress. Tell your partner how sexy he (she) is. Kiss your lover with passion and tenderness. Tell your partner that you're in charge for the evening. Watch the video together, touching each other as you watch. Tell your partner what you want to do to him (her). Get into one of your favorite erotic positions. Give your partner plenty of positive and explicit feedback and finish with loving touches and words.

Fun Dates

- Plan a picnic together.
- Go to an amusement park and hold hands.
- Go to the beach and walk barefoot in the waves.
- Take a bubble bath and paint each other with bubbles.
- Blindfold your partner and take him or her to a favorite place.
- Float with each other in a lake or pool.
- Read each other an erotic, sexy story.

♀ Exercise ♂
Ask for What You Want: Version 2

This exercise takes from thirty minutes to an hour. It should be planned for two nights within a week so that each partner has a turn being the planner. In this version, the active partner will ask to be pleasured in a way that he or she enjoys for up to an hour. The planner will decide who is active and who is passive, or if the activity is mutual. The exercise can be sensual or sexual—anything from a slow foot rub to forty minutes of oral sex. The passive partner does not volunteer anything and does only what the other partner requests. The active partner is in charge of asking for what she or he wants. If the active partner asks for something that the passive partner is not comfortable with, he or she has the right to say no.

Getting into the spirit of the exercise may mean stretching your boundaries a bit. If you are the passive partner, you should be loving and attentive to what your partner wants; you express your vulnerability by being at the other's beck and call. If you are the active partner, you are being vulnerable by asking for what you want. This exercise can have a powerful impact on your relationship. You can and will learn a lot about your partner and yourself.

You can vary this exercise any number of ways, asking for more sweet talk, gentleness, firmness, or specific erotic stimulation. Try to be creative. Listen to your imagination. Be relaxed and have patience with yourself. You might be surprised at how many different activities you'd like to ask for. And, as always, have fun!

Taking Turns This exercise is a shorter version of the one above: it lasts for an hour. You take turns, and you each have half an hour to ask for what you want. This exercise can be done more often, because it does not take much planning or time. Be sure to schedule enough time so each of you can take a turn.

♀ Exercise ♂
Tom Jones Dinner

This exercise has many different names and variations. We chose this one because the scene from the movie of the same title really turned us on. Over the years, we have created our own version of the experience. If you would like to do something differently, go for it! The purpose is to enjoy yourselves while using some of your senses in a different way. You will need some supplies for this event, such as the following:

- Candles
- A warm room or space
- A plastic floor covering
- A variety of finger foods, such as grapes, whipped cream, chicken chunks, cheese, pudding, or any food you crave or find sensual
- A place to shower or hose down afterwards
- Music
- Your sense of humor

As always, be sure to allow plenty of time for your play. The phone should be out of earshot and the kids out of the house (otherwise, try this in a hotel). Choose foods together that you both like, or one of you can surprise the other with extra treats. Set the mood, using candles, music, flowers, or whatever appeals. Lay the plastic covering on the floor, and get undressed or undress each other. Set the finger food around the plastic, being sure to leave room for yourselves. You can rearrange your food as you go.

The rules are simple: you can't feed yourself, and you can't talk. In this exercise you learn to relate to your partner in a nonverbal and primal way. Take turns feeding each other. If you want a particular food, ask for it nonverbally. You can grunt, point, sniff, or beg like a puppy, but you can't talk. You may want to cover a body part of your partner with a food like whipped cream and lick it off.

By the way, making love on the dinner table is acceptable if the mood should strike. A word of caution, though. You should mutually decide in advance if you want sex to be a possibility in the exercise. Sex is not necessary for this to be an intimate, erotic experience. By the way, another advantage to eating this way is that there are no dishes to do. Just roll up the dinner table when you're done!

Trust Exercises That Require Real Trust

People often use the word "trust" as if everyone agrees on the meaning of the word. We define trust as the willingness to let go, because one can honestly say to the other: "I know you have my best interests at heart and regard my needs as at least as important as yours." Such a level of trust requires self-acceptance and genuine acceptance of one's mate.

Although these next exercises require trust, they also call for good sense and appropriate individual boundaries. Always be protective of your core self. If something feels violative, don't override your feelings. Stop. Honor yourself. This is how to protect yourself against abuse.

♀ Exercise ♂
Your Inner Guide

Here is a guided imagery exercise to help you discover healthy boundaries. Take a few deep, relaxing breaths and get comfortable. Take a signal breath to tell your body that you are ready to begin. If you are having trouble relaxing, use one of the relaxation tapes you've already made.

Go to a relaxing, special place in your mind. Allow yourself to become calm and centered by spending some time taking in the details of your special place. Ask an inner guide or other source of inspiration to appear in this place to do this exercise with you. Who is it that appears? Get acquainted with him, her, or it, and spend some time talking together. Your mission is to learn what your boundaries are: What do you need to feel safe? If you have a life motto or a deeply held conviction, what is it?

Take some time to discuss these concepts with your guide. They are critical to having a good relationship with yourself. What is your bottom line on trust? What do you want for yourself? Have your advisor work with you on being able to say no to anything that doesn't feel good to you. Ask your advisor how you can maintain your integrity as an individual while also expanding your trust with your partner. Listen to the answers. Take your time. This is the ultimate in self-talk.

When you've finished your work, make a date with your inner guide to meet again soon. The more you meet, the stronger you'll be, and the more trusting you can learn to become. With clear boundaries, you will be able to take more risks in a relationship without fear of being hurt. When you feel ready to end the exercise, say good-bye to your guide and take a signal breath to tell your body you are finished. Then open your eyes and come back into the here and now.

♀ Exercise ♂
Blind Walk

The blind walk is a therapeutic exercise that has been around for a long time. It is highly effective in helping couples develop trust and intimacy.

In this exercise, take turns being in charge. The passive partner wears a blindfold. The active partner holds the blindfolded partner's hand and takes the partner on a "walk," keeping him (her) safe along the way. The active partner may bring objects for the other to touch or taste, and must be sure to keep the other partner safe at all times.

After fifteen minutes, change roles and repeat the exercise. Afterward, share with each other what it felt like to be in the different roles. If you like, repeat this exercise several times and in different locations. Don't be surprised if you have a new and deeper experience every time!

♀ Exercise ♂
Bondage and Domination

Don't let the title of this exercise cause you to panic! We are not advocating nonconsensual or harmful activities. This exercise does require imagination and some soft restraints, however. Done in a soft, loving manner, this can be a truly erotic and exciting experience. It stretches boundaries and greatly increases trust in each other. Being restrained allows a feeling of letting go that can be awesome.

Do not proceed with this exercise unless you are confident that your partner is able to make your well-being top priority throughout this exercise. If you don't feel that way, we strongly suggest you spend some time figuring out why you don't feel safe with your partner and what you can do together to develop that sense of safety.

If you both feel safe with this, however, take a risk and try this first exercise. Begin by choosing a code word that means the exercise needs to stop *no matter what*. A word such as "red" is a good choice, because it is unrelated to any expression you may utter while in the experience. If your partner hears that word, he or she must remove the restraints; then you both hug and discuss what happened.

Exercise 1 Take turns tying each other's hands with a soft restraint (an old necktie works nicely) for ten minutes each. The untied partner kisses and caresses the tied partner. For the first experience, we recommend nothing too sexual; sensual touches are more appropriate. After ten minutes, switch roles. When the exercise is completed, discuss your experiences with each other. If you are both okay, move on to the next exercise.

Exercise 2 One partner will be in charge for about thirty minutes. If you are the partner in charge, find a place (such as a bedpost) where you can tie your partner's hands down. If you can, restrain the legs also. Remind each other of the signal word. Play with your partner's body, talk sexy, and be creative. Remember, the goal here is to develop intimacy and trust. Don't do anything that will cause your partner to mistrust you. Have fun! Switch roles when the half hour is up, or arrange to switch at another time in the same week.

If the experience has gone well and you want to explore more, you could try a blindfold, different positions, or erotic lingerie. The possibilities are endless. If you find this is an activity you enjoy, you can purchase special equipment, such as leather restraints and silk blindfolds, from stores and mail-order catalogues.

♀ Exercise ♂
The Penile-Vaginal Morse Code Tap

This is a fun and often stimulating side dish during coital sex. When you're ready, stop the thrusting action. Guys, flex your PC muscle. Your penis will flick up and down in her vagina. Gals, do your PC squeezes, which will tighten and loosen your vaginal walls around his erection. When you do it simultaneously, it can be quite a trip. You can also take turns. If you know Morse code, you can tap out "I love you" to each other, or whatever else turns you on.

Switching Focus

We talked a lot about sensate focus and the importance of staying focused in the here and now (see pages 52–54 and 67–68). A more advanced focusing exercise is called the Switching Focus exercise. This was discussed in its basic form in the preliminary exercises in Chapter 5. Here is the full-blown version. When first starting sensate focus, it is easiest to focus on one sensation at a time. Now that you've had some practice, try expanding your repertoire. Switching focus can be tricky, but once you get the hang of it, you will easily incorporate it into your style. You may already be doing it and not even know it.

♀ Exercise ♂
Switching Focus with Yourself

Switching focus is a challenge because it takes concentration. You might find it easiest to practice these skills with your cat, dog, or stuffed animal (the stuffed animal will be more tolerant and cooperative, of course). Start caressing the animal's fur. Take time to really feel the fur and notice its various qualities. Is it soft, coarse, warm, damp, cool, short, long? It may be many of these things. Your goal here is to shift your focus from one of these qualities to another. For example, as you're stroking the fur, first pay attention to its texture (smooth or rough?). Then notice only its temperature (warm, cool, or somewhere in between?). Then move on to its length. The idea is to focus in on only one of these qualities at a time. If this is difficult, spend a little more time with this, maybe fifteen minutes. Use encouraging self-talk if you begin to get frustrated. Have patience. This is not easy.

♀ Exercise ♂
Switching Focus with Your Partner

Meet at a prime time for this exercise. By that we mean when you both can be alert, clearheaded, and free from other distractions. Since this is a difficult exercise, let each other know you will be patient. You may want to set a mood that feels comfortable and relaxed. Get undressed and lie next to each other. We suggest you hug and kiss before beginning.

Using massage oil, each of you will place your hand on your partner's genitals. Slowly caress and focus on the sensation of how your partner's genitals feel for several minutes. Now focus on how your genitals feel being caressed by your partner. Can you switch back and forth between the two sensations, first concentrating on one, then the other? Take your time, use some positive self-talk, and breathe.

Next, switch your focus to how your hand feels touching your partner's genitals, that is, focus on the sensations in your hand, not on his genitals. Then switch your focus to the feeling of how your partner's hand feels touching your genitals!

Do we have you totally confused? There are actually four different sensations. Can you separate them? Don't give up! Once you can focus on such subtle differences, your sex life will never be the same. This is advanced stuff, so don't be discouraged. When you think you have it, try the next exercise, which will be really fun if you both like oral sex. The ultimate treat, once you master the individual sensations and the general concept of switching focus, is to put the sensations together in combinations of two or more. Imagine the possibilities—the flavors, feelings, and emotions you can enjoy—as you experiment like a master chef of love with a new array of spices.

♀ Exercise ♂
Switching Focus with Your Partner during Mutual Oral Sex

If you have been using oil, you may want to shower. We suggest showering anyway, because oral sex is often most appealing when you both smell clean. Again, make sure you have quality time set aside for this exercise, and hug and kiss before beginning. Switching focus during mutual oral sex can be dramatic.

To begin, each of you will use sensate focus to notice how your partner's genitals feel. Really feel them in your mouth. The idea is to focus on how your partner's genitals feel to you, not to your partner.

Now focus on the feelings and sensations in your own genitals. It may seem really hard to switch, but you can do it.

Next, switch your focus to how your mouth and tongue feel. Can you feel the ridges, the hardness, the softness in your mouth?

Switch to noticing how your partner's mouth and tongue feel. What is that like?

If you can, shift your focus to other sensations, such as odor and taste, then back to touch, and see if you can experience these sensations in various combinations. This exercise can help you really understand what switching focus means. When you think you've got it, try switching focus in other areas of your life. It can bring new and enlightening dimensions to everything you do.

The Final Six

The following six exercises all have something in common: each, in its unique way, will help the two of you achieve a deeper bond. These exercises require and further develop mutual trust, respect, and commitment. As you get to know yourselves and each other more wholly, not only will the experience of your orgasms be simultaneous in nature, but also the enjoyment of your relationship. This state of harmonious togetherness, according to the nature of who we are as gendered beings, is what we refer to as *relationship simultaneity*.

♀ Exercise ♂
Nonverbal Communication Using Your Hands

While we were doing our training in the seventies, our mentor, Barbara Roberts, taught us this exercise, which helps promote mutuality and intimacy. It is very effective, since it requires you to focus on your sense while paying attention to each other.

First, make a tape recording. When recording, take turns saying the following list of ten words, leaving a thirty-second pause between words. You can add any words that have meaning for either of you.

- Hello
- Happy
- Shy
- Sexy

- Assertive
- Loving
- Angry
- Passive
- Anxious
- Proud
- Goodbye

After recording the words, record soft music that you both like. The music should play for about one minute.

The exercise itself is like a hand dance. Sit across from your partner in a comfortable position. Chairs are good, or you can sit cross-legged on the floor. Close your eyes and lightly touch your hands to your partner's hands, palms together. Start the tape. As you hear each word, let your hands express the feeling the word invokes to your partner's hands. See how similar your movements are. When the music starts to play, "dance" with your hands until the end of the exercise. You may become frustrated the first time you do this exercise, and it may take several tries before you both get in synch. Be patient and loving with each other. Observe your interaction, and notice, among other things, the following:

- Is one of you more assertive?
- Are you willing to feel each other's feelings?
- Can you find a simultaneous hand movement?
- Are you being respectful of each other?

Remember, there are no leaders or followers, no winners or losers in this exercise. It takes two to tango.

♀ Exercise ♂
Mutual Masturbation: Pleasing Yourself—Together

Remember our discussions on masturbation? Guess what? Here you go again! Although we know it isn't easy to overcome years of conditioning, we hope you have both let go of any shame you have felt about self-satisfaction. Again we ask that you give your inhibitions a push. In two of the exercises that follow, you and your partner will masturbate together. It may seem embarrassing and strange, but the experience can also be erotic and intimate. We ask you to take some risks and do these exercises so you can grow together sexually. Take ten to fifteen minutes for each exercise.

Exercise 1 This is similar to the switching focus exercises you have already done. Lie next to your partner and caress her or his genitals; your partner will do the same to you. While you do this, switch focus back and forth from your partner to you, from your hand to your genitals.

Exercise 2 Lie next to your partner. This time, start by caressing your own genitals. Practice switching focus, but mostly keep your focus on yourself.

Exercise 3 Lie next to your partner as both of you begin to masturbate. As you caress yourself, watch your partner. Allow yourself to experience your partner turning himself or herself on. This experience takes love, patience, trust, and caring.

Exercise 4 In this exercise, you will take turns masturbating. As one of you masturbates, the other watches without doing any self-pleasuring. The person who is self-pleasuring can feel very vulnerable doing this. Make sure you are both supportive of each other. If you are the person who is self-pleasuring, you can choose to come to orgasm or not, then switch roles when you feel complete. This experience can be very erotic and powerful for both of you.

Exploring Fantasies Together

Everyone has fantasies. Nancy Friday's books have been invaluable in helping women give themselves permission to explore some of theirs. Not all fantasies are sexual, of course; daydreams of any kind are fantasies. A fantasy is your imagination operating without restraint, and it often enters the mind uninvited. Anything is possible in fantasy, from the utterly romantic to the tinglingly erotic. Some people's sexual fantasies are just about breasts or penises, while others have elaborate fantasies. Some story lines may revolve around acts considered taboo in our culture.

The exercises below involve sharing your fantasies with your partner. We want you to start with the clear idea that there is nothing wrong with fantasy. The potential problem that can arise with fantasy is in acting it out. If you are not sure of the difference between fantasizing and acting out, we suggest you seek help from a qualified mental health professional.

There are different ways to share a fantasy with your partner. The first rule is, be respectful. A fantasy about someone other than your partner doesn't mean that you don't love him or her, but it might be helpful to share this information in a sensitive manner. At the same time, try not to take your partner's fantasies about others as a negative reflection on you; they are really just the opposite. If your partner feels safe enough to share fantasies, it means your partner trusts you deeply. It is important to maintain an open and loving attitude while your partner is sharing his or her most intimate, private thoughts.

When your partner shares a fantasy with you, there are several things that can happen:

- It may turn you on
- It may turn you off
- It may upset you
- You may be embarrassed
- You may feel closer to your mate

As this could be a brand new experience for one or both of you, let's start with easy steps and build mutual fantasies.

♀ Exercise ♂
Individual Fantasy Exercise

Recall a fantasy or daydream you have had. Write it down in as much detail as you can.

Do you fantasize when you masturbate? If so, what are those fantasies like? Write them down.

Do you fantasize during intercourse? About what or whom? Also write this down. Don't forget the details. Keep a journal of these fantasies and add to it when you imagine new ones or variations. Reread it occasionally, and if a comfortable time should occur, consider sharing one or more fantasies with your partner.

♀ Exercise ♂
Sharing a Fantasy with Your Partner

Some people worry that if they share a fantasy it will no longer be special. That may be true, but we urge you to take a risk and do it anyway. Sharing it may actually make the fantasy better.

For the first fantasy exercise, ask your partner to participate in a sexual or sensual experience you have wanted to try and have been afraid to ask for. Set a special time to meet when you will each take a turn to ask for a fantasy activity. Remember, the fantasy should be something to which you're pretty certain your partner would not object (whipped cream or playacting might be okay, but having sex with your partner's sibling might not). Be sensitive to your partner's need for safety and comfort, or this exercise won't work.

Again, make sure you have quality time set aside, and choose who will go first. Get comfortable! If you are the one describing the fantasy, start with hugs and kisses, telling your partner how much you love him or her and how much you appreciate your partner's willingness to listen. Describe your fantasy in as much detail as possible. Hug and caress each other as you share. Your partner should make no comment but just listen. After you have shared the fantasy, you can both tell each other of your love and do some gentle caressing. You might even make love if both of you are inclined. Make sure you do this exercise again in a day or two, reversing roles, so both of you have equal time.

Afterwards, share your experiences or write in your journal for yourself. Understand that such sharing is meant to enhance your relationship, not erode it. Be respectful and sensitive about your partner's feelings and needs. If clear problems arise, we suggest you seek help from a counselor or other qualified mental health professional. Ideally, you will both develop an erotic, enjoyable activity as part of your lovemaking from this exercise.

We are often asked about the pros and cons of fantasizing during lovemaking. In general, whenever one (or both) partner(s) fantasizes silently, there is a loss of couple intimacy and erotic connection to one's partner. The erotic triggers become individual and external to the relationship. On the other hand, a sex therapist will occasionally recommend such individual silent fantasies as part of a specialized therapeutic exercise for a particular problem. There are two ways fantasies occur during lovemaking. The first way is in silence, sometimes at a therapist's recommendation, as was just described. The second way is when the fantasies are open and shared and are made part of a couple's activity. We normally recommend that couples seeking greater intimacy focus on the here and now experience with their partners and verbally share their erotic thoughts.

♀ Exercise ♂
Erotic Activities and Fantasies

There are many ways to explore what you both find erotic without fantasies being the focus. In fact, such exploration can be a fantasy come true. We feel erotic activities put spark in a relationship and keep those juices flowing. Here are a few examples.

The Restaurant Experience Go out to a really nice restaurant together. Choose a place that is elegant and dressy. Don't wear any underwear. Be aware all evening that you're both naked under those elegant clothes, and allow yourselves to feel aroused knowing you can't act on those feelings while in the restaurant. When you get home, watch out!

The Drive-in Experience If there is still a drive-in theater where you live, go to a movie and make out. Feel each other up, but don't have sex. Just grope and feel and explore, and steam up those windows!

Remote Control Buy a remote control vibrator or one with a long wire. One of you will wear it, while the other control it. Go to brunch or a movie. The partner wearing the vibrator will never know when a vibration is coming.

Body Painting Purchase body paints and take turns painting each other's body. This can get very erotic. Take your time with the brush. Make sure you have a place to wash off.

Outdoor Sex This activity is not for the faint of heart. Many of our clients have told us of experiences in which they find a remote spot outdoors to have sex. The excitement is in the possibility of being caught. This must be done by mutual consent.

Vegetarian Sex You know all the jokes about cucumbers. If you're game, try inserting some safe but interesting vegetables into different orifices. *Caution:* if you do anything anal, make sure the object you use has a long, perpendicular stop piece. The anus can literally suck an object in, and most anal plugs have a T-bar on them. You wouldn't like to end up in the emergency room having something removed.

♀ Exercise ♂
Stream of Consciousness:
The Ultimate Trust and Intimacy Builder

A simultaneous orgasm is an uninhibited flow of basic sexual energy as part of human fusion. "Stream of consciousness" is its verbal counterpart. The phrase was used to describe a style of writing created by the author James Joyce, demonstrated beautifully in his novel, *Ulysses*. In that work a stream of consciousness, or flow of thoughts, with a highly erotic slant is heard through the voice of Molly Bloom. Molly's thoughts tumble out unedited so the reader can get inside her head.

Stream of consciousness is very different from normal conversation, in which we edit what we are going to say before the words are spoken. Editing has two uses. First, speech comes out in an intelligible manner. Second, it is screened for content and appropriateness. It would be a highly volatile and perhaps dangerous world if we all went around saying whatever was in our minds.

Edited output and stream of consciousness are concepts that can also be applied to nonverbal expression, such as dance or music. In dance, we can engage in choreographed dance movements or simply flow with the mood and environment. In music, we can play the notes in front of us or we can improvise. Similarly, in our sex lives, we may stick to a familiar though enjoyable routine, or we can be spontaneous and try something new with less predictable results.

Stream of consciousness is risky, and a high degree of trust is necessary before reaching this level of interaction. It is an exercise that is difficult to master, so stay with it until you've got it, which may take several tries. The process builds on an already existing measure of simultaneity and intimacy. At our clinic, we use Stream of Consciousness with a Basic Genital Caress, although stream of consciousness can be used with any form of stimulation, from a basic caress to intercourse. We only do this exercise with couples who are in relationships that are stable, solid, and can handle waves. The results can be spectacular.

After some warm-up, one partner begins by caressing the other's genitals and continues for about fifteen or twenty minutes. If you are the partner receiving the caress, start speaking almost immediately, saying whatever comes to mind; allow your speech to flow spontaneously, stream-of-consciousness fashion, so you hear it at the same time as your partner. Whatever comes, comes. It may be physical expression, actual words, or noise—sometimes comprehensible, sometimes not. It may be funny, erotic, pleasant, nonsensical, or even hostile, sometimes even toward your partner. Whatever comes out, the caressing partner needs to stay focused on not taking anything personally, just letting you do your thing.

We have watched many couples do this exercise repeatedly, then finally break through with genuine, unedited communication. If you are at all unsure, stop at any point in the exercise, or don't try it at all. If you are seeing a therapist, we strongly urge you to consult him or her before trying this.

As a preliminary exercise, you can practice stream of consciousness by speaking aloud to yourself or by writing in a completely spontaneous and unedited fashion. We do this all the time during the night when dreaming, and you know what kinds of images that produces. In fact, stream of consciousness could also be called a waking dream. Some people enjoy this form of self-revelation by closing their eyes, examining the inside of their eyelids, and allowing images to emerge. If you are relaxed when you do this, colors, patterns, and movement will appear from the darkness. This can be a profound and personal spiritual experience.

・ ・ ・

Well, you have arrived at the last page, but the journey is not over. Here are our thanks to you for reading this book, thinking about the ideas, trying the exercises, and enjoying the results. Which parts were fun, scary, interesting, tough, enlightening, or exciting? Which do you want to further explore or quietly digest? What new adventures do you have in mind for yourself and each other? Let us know.

The process from conception to creation to the publishing of this book have taken us through the normal human cycles of hope, despair, problems, opportunity, and accomplishment. Ultimately, because we cared for each other along the way, this experience brought us closer together. Since we now command and share more of what nature provided for our sexual pleasure, we can say:

It was good for us. Was it good for you? We hope so.

Anita and Michael

Bibliography

Barbach, L. *For Yourself: The Fulfillment of Female Sexuality*. New York: Doubleday, 1975.

Batten, M. *Sexual Strategies: How Females Choose Their Mates*. New York: Tarcher/Putnam, 1992.

The Boston Women's Health Book Collective. *The New Our Bodies, Ourselves*. New York: Touchstone, 1984.

Dodson, B. *Sex for One: The Joy of Selfloving*. New York: Crown Trade Paperbacks, 1987.

Federation of Feminist Women's Health Centers. *A New View of a Woman's Body*. West Hollywood, CA: Feminist Health Press, 1991.

Friday, N. *Women On Top: How Real Life Has Changed Women's Sexual Fantasies*. New York: Simon & Schuster, 1991.

Grant, T. *Being a Woman: Fulfilling Your Femininity and Finding Love*. New York: Avon Books, 1988.

Keesling, B. *Sexual Healing: A Self-Help Program to Enhance Your Sensuality and Overcome Common Sexual Problems*. Claremont, CA: Hunter House, 1990.

Kline-Graber, G. & Graber, B. *Woman's Orgasm: A Guide to Sexual Satisfaction*. New York: Warner, 1975.

Ladas, A. K., Whipple, B. & Perry, J. D. *The G Spot: and Other Recent Discoveries About Human Sexuality*. New York: Dell, 1982.

Masters, W. H. & Johnson, V. E. *Human Sexual Response*. New York: Bantam, 1966.

Pollard, J. K. *Self-Parenting: The Complete Guide to Your Inner Conversations*. Malibu, CA: Generic Human Studies Publishing, 1987.

Riskin, M. *Stop In The Name Of Love: Ejaculation Control For Life*. Whittier, CA: Choice Publishing, 1994.

Robinson, M. *The Power of Sexual Surrender*. New York: Doubleday and Company, 1959.

Rossman, M. L. *Healing Yourself: A Step-By-Step Program For Better Health Through Imagery*. New York: Pocket Books, 1987.

Sevely, J. L. *Eve's Secrets: A New Theory of Female Sexuality*. New York: Random House, 1987.

Stewart, J. *The Complete Manual of Sexual Positions: A Sensual Guide to Lovemaking*. Chatsworth, CA: Media Press, 1990.

Stuart, R. B. & Jacobson, B. *Weight, Sex, & Marriage: A Delicate Balance*. New York: Norton, 1995.

Tannahill, R. *Sex in History*. New York: Stein & Day, 1992.

Yapko, M. D. *Trancework: An Introduction to the Practice of Clinical Hypnosis*. New York: Brunner/Mazel, 1990.

Zilbergeld, B. *The New Male Sexuality: The Truth About Men, Sex, and Pleasure*. New York: Bantam, 1992.

Recommended Reading

Nonfiction

Anand, Margo. *The Art of Sexual Magic.* New York: Putnam, 1996. If you are interested in tantra and the power of sexuality, here is an enchanting book on how to channel the power of sexual energy beyond lovemaking. Anand's previous book, *The Art of Sexual Ecstasy* (New York: Putnam/Tarcher, 1991), explains tantra for Western couples.

Arava, Douglas Abrams and Mantak Chia. *The Multi-Orgasmic Man: Sexual Secrets Every Man Should Know.* San Francisco: HarperCollins, 1996. Here are simple physical and psychological techniques for men, including more details on how to have those fabulous multiple orgasms.

Barbach, Lonnie, M.D. *For Yourself.* New York: Doubleday, 1976.
A classic for women of all ages, this reassuring book helps women discover, and truly appreciate, their sexual self.

Block, Joel D., Ph.D. *Secrets of Better Sex.* Englewood Cliffs, NJ: Prentice Hall, 1996.
With this fun A–Z style book, you can dip in and out, to expand your sexual knowledge as you fancy.

Comfort, Alex. *The New Joy of Sex.* New York: Crown, 1991.
This fully updated edition of the classic offers explicit advice for couples and singles today. If you're looking for variety, check this out, but we recommend you do so after you have mastered the pleasures of sensate focus.

Davis, Elizabeth. *Women, Sex and Desire: Understanding Your Sexuality at Every Stage of Life.* Alameda, CA: Hunter House, 1995.
An insightful look at women's sexuality from puberty to pregnancy, midlife, menopause, and beyond.

Engel, Beverly, Ph.D. *Raising Your Sexual Self-Esteem: How to Feel Better About Your Sexuality and Yourself.* New York: Fawcett Books, 1995. Solid, positive advice and encouragement from an expert on women's relationship issues. An especially helpful book for women who have experienced abuse and for their partners.

Fischer, Lynn. *The Better Sex Diet: The Medically Based Low-Fat Eating Plan for Increased Sexual Vitality In Just 6 Weeks.* Washington, DC: Living Planet, 1996.
The author draws from authoritative scientific data and expertise in low-fat cooking to create an effective, six-week plan that will increase sexual potency.

Friday, Nancy. *Men in Love: Men's Sexual Fantasies: The Triumph of Love Over Rage.* New York: Dell, 1992.

Gillette, Douglas and Robert Moore. *The Lover Within: Accessing the Lover in the Male Psyche.* New York: Avon Books, 1995.

Jacobowitz, Ruth S. *150 Most-Asked Questions About Midlife Sex, Love, and Intimacy: What Women and Their Partners Really Want to Know.* New York: Hearst Books, 1995.
Wondering what's on every other couple's mind? This book tells you, and answers all questions in a friendly, down-to-earth manner.

Keesling, Barbara, Ph.D. *Sexual Healing: How Good Loving is Good for You—and Your Relationship.* Alameda, CA: Hunter House, 1996.
Here is a more enjoyable prescription for healing—a look at how sex and sexual intimacy can lead to improved physical and mental health.

Keesling, Barbara, Ph.D. *Sexual Pleasure: Reaching New Heights of Sexual Arousal and Intimacy.* Alameda, CA: Hunter House, 1993.
A great step-by-step approach to developing sensual awareness, trust, intimacy, and deeper desire. Dr. Keesling calls on the sensate–focus style to take you to the heights of arousal and intimacy.

Lloyd-Elliot, Martin. *Secrets of Sexual Body Language.* Berkeley, CA: Ulysses Press, 1996.
An interesting book with insights into how we speak the languages of love and seduction—without words.

Purvis, Kenneth, M.D., Ph.D. *The Male Sexual Machine: An Owner's Manual.* New York: St. Martin's Press, 1993.

Stoppard, Miriam, M.D. *The Magic of Sex.* New York: Dorling-Kindersley, 1992.
Although prescriptive at times, this book provides helpful "sexual profile" questionnaires; discussion openers; techniques; and solid information on physical, psychological, and medical problems.

Fiction

Baker, Nicholson. *Vox: A Novel.* New York: Vintage, 1995.
This is the book that made phone sex famous. Written in the form of a phone conversation, it explores the boundaries of fantasy, foreplay, and sex. Baker is known most recently for his erotic novel, *The Fermata* (New York: Vintage, 1995).

Bell, Roseann P., Miriam Decosta-Willis, and Donald Martin, eds. *Erotique Noire: Black Erotica.* New York: Anchor Books, 1992.
This collection of short stories, poems, folk tales, and letters celebrates Black erotica, from the lyrical to the lascivious. It includes such well-known authors as Alice Walker, Ntozake Shange, and Barbara Chase-Riboud, among others.

Bright, Susie, ed. *The Best American Erotica, 1995.* New York: Touchstone Books, 1995.
An exceptional collection of erotica, featuring works by such well-known writers as Nicholson Baker and Robert Olen Butler, as well as by new voices. Other Best American collections include those of 1994 and 1996.

Bright, Susie ed. *Herotica.* San Francisco: Down There Press, 1993.
Now considered an underground classic, this collection of erotica written by women cuts across sexual preference, from "vanilla sex" to S&M. If you like this collection, check out the Herotica collections 2, 3, and 4.

Miller, Henry. *Tropic of Cancer*. New York: Grove Press, 1989.
This autobiographical piece, banned in the United States until 1961, celebrates the profligate life of an expatriate in Paris. Henry Miller's unapologetic sexual frankness opened the door for today's erotica. Other Miller favorites include *Tropic of Capricorn* (New York: Grove Press, 1987) and *Crazy Cock* (New York: Grove Press, 1992).

Nin, Anaïs. *Delta of Venus*. New York: Harcourt-Brace, 1977.
A classic rich in sensual curiosity, passion, and driving desire that made Anaïs Nin famous. If you find pleasure in Nin's distinctive writing, dip into her extensive diaries for details of her real-life sexual explorations.

Pond, Lily and Richard Russo, eds. *Yellow Silk: Erotic Arts and Letters*. New York: Random House, 1992.
A compendium of superb erotic literature and artwork for both men and women, drawn from the literary erotic magazine of the same title. *The Book of Eros: Art and Letters from Yellow Silk* (New York: Crown, 1996) is a newly released, follow-up anthology and *Yellow Silk* itself is a quarterly publication.

Rice, Anne (as Anne Rampling). *Belinda*. New York: Jove Publications, 1994.
A controversial tale of seduction and obsession, written by the bestselling author of the *Vampire Chronicles* under a pseudonym. If you enjoy Rice's erotica, try venturing into her darker Sleeping Beauty series.

Slung, Michele, ed. *Fever: Sensual Stories by Women Writers*. San Francisco: HarperCollins, 1995.
There's something in this collection for everyone—from young to old, romantic to adventurous, solo to multiple. Slung's first book of erotica was *Slow Hand: Women Writing Erotica* (New York: HarperPerennial, 1993).

Resources

For information about sex therapy or to find a board certified sex therapist:

> Contact the **American Association of Sex Educators, Counselors, and Therapists** (AASECT) by mail at P.O. Box 238, Mount Vernon, IA 52314-0208 or by e-mail at CompuServe (GO HSXTOP).

> Contact the **American Board of Sexology** (ABS) by calling the executive director at 202-462-2122 or visit its web site at http://www.mental-health.com/PsychScapes.

For more information about guided imagery:

> Contact the **Academy for Guided Imagery** (AGI) by mail at P.O. Box 2070, Mill Valley, CA 94942.

For information about marriage, family, and child counselors (MFCC) or to find a qualified MFCC:

> Contact the **National Association of Marriage and Family Therapists** (NAMFT) by phone at 202-452-0109 or by mail at 1133 15th Street NW, Suite 300, Washington, DC 23305-3700.

To find erotic reading or videos and quality sexual aids:

> Contact **Good Vibrations/The Sexuality Library** by telephone at 800-289-8423 or by mail at 938 Howard Street, Suite 101, San Francisco, CA 94103.

For more information about sexuality and research on sexuality:

> Contact the **Society for the Scientific Study of Sexuality** (SSSS) by mail at P.O. Box 208, Mount Vernon, IA 52314-0208 or visit its web site at http://www.ssc.wisc.edu/ssss/membership.htm.

Appendix

Five Patterns of Arousal and Orgasm

Graphically displayed in the figures below are five typical patterns of arousal and orgasm that are similar among men and women. They are measured on a 1–10 scale, with 1 indicating no arousal whatsoever and 10 meaning orgasm. They can be plotted over time measured in minutes. When patterns 3, 4, and 5 become achievable by both partners, the joy of simultaneous orgasm is more easily experienced.

Each of these graphs shows arousal levels plotted against elapsed time.

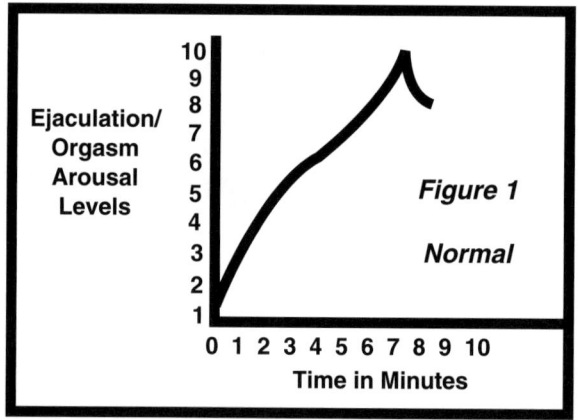

Figure One The classic Masters and Johnson "normal ejaculatory pattern" which is still valid today.

This is a man who maintains his erection for about seven minutes of sustained stimulation during intercourse and then ejaculates. It is also a typical pattern for a woman who orgasms during intercourse.

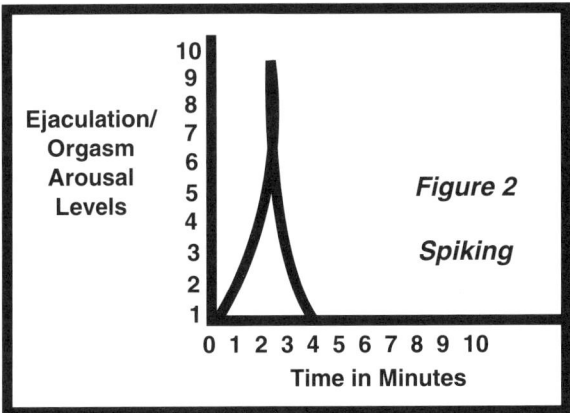

Figure Two The pattern of a man with premature ejaculation. His arousal "spikes up" rapidly to an ejaculation, with up to two minutes of stimulation. In some extreme cases, the ejaculation may occur right at or even before the moment of vaginal penetration. The pattern is reversible in virtually all men who diligently follow the instructions. This also demonstrates the pattern of a woman who manifests the rare condition of premature orgasm.

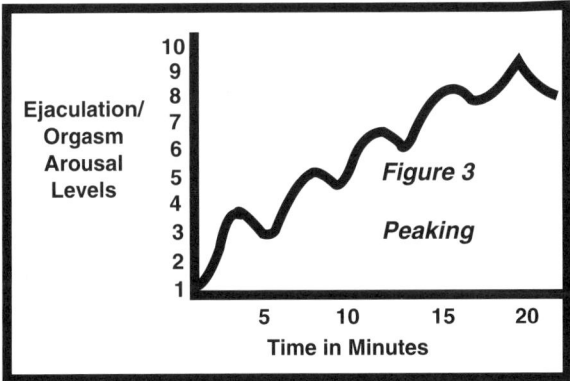

Figure Three The pattern of a man or woman who is "peaking." In this pattern, one's arousal goes up and down in a series of controllable peaks and valleys, or waves. When peaking is mastered, one can last essentially as long as one wishes, climaxing when one wishes to.

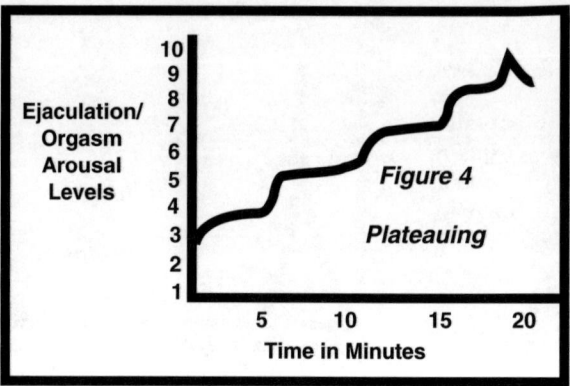

Figure Four The pattern of a person who is "plateauing." A plateau is an extended peak, and once this skill is learned, one can remain at a very high level of arousal indefinitely, then climax, or even go into a peaking pattern if she or he prefers.

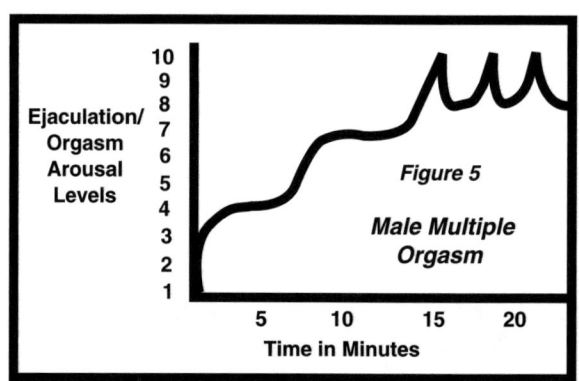

Figure Five The pattern of a man who has learned to achieve two or more non-ejaculatory orgasms, combined with his choice of peaks or plateaus. This is also the pattern of a woman who can equally achieve multiple orgasms, though her time frame is subject to variation.

Index

A

adolescent sexuality, exploring, 43–52
anal intercourse, 177
arousal awareness, 84–85
Arousal Awareness "Squeeze" (exercise for men), 86
arousal levels, men, 84–86, 214–216; women, 130–131, 214–216
Ask for What You Want (exercise): Version 1, 188–190; Version 2, 190–191
Ask Your Partner for More Support (exercise), 153–154
Assiagoli, Robert, 12
attitudes about sex, 26–29, 71–74, 120

B

Back Caress (exercise), 54–55
Basic Arousal Awareness à Deux (exercise for men), 89–90
Basic Genital Caress (exercise for men), 82–84
Beauvoir, Simone de, 141
biological imperatives, 14, 15
birth control pills, 73
Blind Walk (exercise), 193–194
Bondage and Domination (exercise), 194–195
bonding, 13–14, 16, 41
brain and sex, 67
breathing, 81–82

C

Chesser, Eustace, 34
childbirth and orgasms, 115, 134–135
Climbing Higher and Higher with Your PC "Brake" (exercise for men), 94–95
clitoris, 117, 124
Cognitive Steps to Greater Sexual Freedom (exercise for women), 120–121
coital alignment technique, 42
Comfort, Alex, 35
commitment, 18
Conscious Breathing (exercise), 68–69
cortex, 67
Creating Plateaus with Your Partner (exercise), 102–103
Crete, 11–12

D

desire, 16, 60–61, 73
diet, 62
dildos, 126
Distract the Distraction (exercise for women), 138–139
Dress Rehearsal (exercise), 169–171

E

Eichel, Edward, 42
Eisler, Riane, 11
Ejaculation Awareness with Your Partner (exercise for men), 157

ejaculation, 91–92, 155, 156; premature, 26, 28, 41, 80–81, 100, 215; rapid, 80
ejaculatory control, 91–111, 146, 155–163
ejaculatory orgasm, women, 56, 117, 125, 129, 134–135, 142–143
Elders, Jocelyn, 32
emotionality, 8
equality, 19
erections, 41, 100, 155; difficulties, 41, 100
Erotic Activities and Fantasies (exercise), 203–204
erotica, 34
estrogen, 8, 61, 64
exercises for men or women: Conscious Breathing, 68–69; Exploring Your Adolescent Sexuality, 43–48; Grounding, 69; Individual Fantasy Exercise, 202; Pelvic Thrusts and Rolls, 65; Switching Focus with Yourself, 196
exercises for men: Arousal Awareness "Squeeze," 86; Basic Arousal Awareness à Deux, 89–90; Basic Genital Caress, 82–84; Climbing Higher and Higher with Your PC "Brake," 94–95; Ejaculation Awareness with Your Partner, 157; Learning to Peak, 87–88; Multiple Orgasm with Your Partner, 160–161; Partner Peaking: An Advanced Variation, 96–97; Peaking with a Partner: Part Two, 95–96; Peaking with the PC Muscle by Yourself, 92–93; Peaking with the PC Muscle Your Way, 93–94; Plateauing by Yourself, 97–98; Plateauing by Yourself: PC Squeeze, 98; Plateauing by Yourself: Switching Strokes, 99; Solo Ejaculation Awareness, 157; Solo Multiple Orgasm, 159–160; Start and Stop: Peaking with a Partner, 90–91; Tuning in to Your Arousal, 85
exercises for partners: Ask for What You Want: Version 1, 188–190; Ask for What You Want: Version 2, 190–191; Ask Your Partner for More Support, 153–154; Back Caress, 54–55; Blind Walk, 193–194; Bondage and Domination, 194–195; Dress Rehearsal, 169–171; Erotic Activities and Fantasies, 203–204; Exploring Your Adolescent Sexuality as a Couple: Part One, 48–50; Exploring Your Adolescent Sexuality as a Couple: Part Two, 51–52; Making the Multiple Simultaneous Orgasm, 181–182; Multiple Orgasms with Intercourse, 153; Mutual Masturbation: Pleasing Yourself—Together, 200; Nonverbal Communication Using Your Hands, 198–199; PC Squeeze, 65; Penile-Vaginal Morse Code Tap, 195; Practicing with Your Partner, 152–153; Sharing a Fantasy with Your Partner, 202–203; Side to Side Loving, 104–105; Stream of Consciousness: The

Ultimate Trust and Intimacy Builder, 204–206; Switching Focus with Your Partner, 196–197; Switching Focus with Your Partner During Mutual Oral Sex, 197–198; Tensing/Relaxing, 69; Tom Jones Dinner, 191–192; Your Inner Guide, 193

exercises for women: Cognitive Steps to Greater Sexual Freedom, 120–121; Fake It till You Make It, 136–137; High Rider, 139–140; Peaking and Plateauing, 132–134; Reconnecting with Sexuality, Reawakening Desire, 118–120; Sensate Focus in Service of the Multiple Orgasm, 149–150; Towel Over His Face, 137–138; Vaginal Orgasms, 127–129

expectations, 72

Exploring Your Adolescent Sexuality (exercise), 43–48

Exploring Your Adolescent Sexuality as a Couple (exercise): Part One, 48–50; Part Two, 51–52

F

Fake It till You Make It (exercise for women), 136–137
fantasies, 201–206
femininity, 14, 15
fertilization, 2
focus, switching, 101–103, 195–198
food and sex, 62, 63–64, 191–192
Friday, Nancy, 33, 201

G

gender differences, 15–18, 30, 31; acknowledgment of, 12
Good Vibrations, 126
Grey, Alexander, 175
Grounding (exercise), 69
G-spot, 125, 129
G-spot orgasm, 56, 117, 129, 134–135, 142–143

H

Hawkes, Jacquetta, 12
High Rider (exercise for women), 139–140
hormonal levels, 64
hormones, 73
hovering, 167, 169–172

I

impotence, 27
Individual Fantasy Exercise (exercise), 202
infidelity, 18
inorgasmia, 28, 30, 41
instinctual self, 11

J

Jong, Erica, 141
joy spots, 123–125
Joyce, James, 205

K

Kinsey Institute, 26
kissing, 53, 54

L

labia, 117
Lawrence, D. H., 36, 141

Learning to Peak (exercise for men), 87–88
Leonard, George, 35
libido, 73, 81

M

Making the Multiple Simultaneous Orgasm (exercise), 181–182
marriage, models of, 13
masculinity, 14–16
Massage (exercise), 70
Masters and Johnson, 29–30, 214
masturbation, 32–33, 45–47; mutual, 56, 176; women and, 116
Moonstruck, 16
Multiple Orgasm with Your Partner (exercise for men), 160–161
Multiple Orgasms with Intercourse (exercise), 153
multiple orgasms, female, 132–134, 147–155
multiple orgasms, male, 56, 146, 155–163
Mutual Masturbation: Pleasing Yourself—Together (exercise), 200
mutual pleasuring, 176

N

Nin, Anaïs, 35
nipples, 117
nondemand interaction, 67
Nonverbal Communication Using Your Hands (exercise), 198–199
nutrition, 62

O

Ogden, Gina, 117
oral sex, 176–177; mutual, 56
orgasm and fertilization, 2
orgasms, difficulty with, 28, 30, 41, 115–116
orgasms, ejaculatory, 125, 129, 134–135
orgasms, female, biological purpose, 2; G-spot, 56, 117, 129, 134–135, 142–143; multiple, 41, 117, 146–163; physiology of, 116–117, 214–216; strategies for achieving multiple, 148–149
orgasms, G-spot, 56, 117, 129, 134–135, 142–143
orgasms, male, biological purpose, 2; multiple, 146, 155–163, 216
orgasms, multiple, 41, 117, 146–163
orgasms, multiple simultaneous, 181–182
orgasms, patterns of, 214–216
orgasms, simultaneous, biological purpose, 2–3
orgasms, triggering, 167–168, 173–175
orgasms, nonejaculatory, male, 156
ovum, 3

P

Partner Peaking: An Advanced Variation (exercise), 96–97
PC muscle, 64, 82, 91–97, 128, 156; exercises, 27, 65, 166
PC Squeeze (exercise), 65
peaking, 41, 86–87, 92–94, 215
Peaking and Plateauing (exercise for women), 132–134
Peaking with a Partner: Part Two (exercise), 95–96
Peaking with the PC Muscle by Yourself (exercise for men), 92–93

Peaking with the PC Muscle Your Way (exercise for men), 93–94
Pelvic Thrusts and Rolls (exercise), 65
Penile-Vaginal Morse Code Tap (exercise), 195
penis size, 29
performance anxiety, 3, 27
plateauing, 41, 97–100, 131, 216
Plateauing by Yourself (exercise for men), 97–98
Plateauing by Yourself: Changing Your Focus (exercise for men), 99
Plateauing by Yourself: PC Squeeze (exercise for men), 98
Plateauing by Yourself: Switching Strokes (exercise for men), 99
Plateauing with Intercourse (exercise), 108–109
play, 111, 186–192
Pollard, John, 73, 74
positions, sex, 104–109
post-coital pleasures, 162–163, 182–183
power, male 16–17
power-cherish dynamic, 16, 18
Practicing with Your Partner (exercise), 152–153
premature ejaculation, 26, 28, 41, 80–81, 100, 215
progesterone, 61
pubococcygeus (PC) muscle (see PC muscle)

R

rapid ejaculation, 80
Reconnecting with Sexuality, Reawakening Desire (exercise for women), 118–120
refractory period, 42, 155
Reich, Wilhelm, 66
relaxation, 40, 44, 66, 68–70
respect, 16–17
Reyes, Alina, 36
Rice, Alice, 37
Ross, Francesca, 36

S

self-affirmation, 74
Self-Parenting: The Complete Guide to Your Inner Conversations, 73, 74
semen, 156
Sensate Focus in the Service of the Multiple Orgasm (exercise for women), 149–150
sensate focus, 30, 52–54, 88, 66–67, 149–150
sensation management, 100–102
sensual touch, 41
sex therapy industry, 26–27, 29–30
sex toys, 126
sexual appetite, 60–61
sexual dissatisfaction, 4
sexual exploration, 4
sexual identity, 117
sexual styles, 5, 177–180
sexuality, beliefs about, 26–29, 71–74, 120
sexuality, scientific era of, 31–32
sexuality, women's, 146–147
shame, 47, 71–72
Sharing a Fantasy with Your Partner (exercise), 202–203
Side to Side Loving (exercise), 104–105
simultaneous orgasm, controlling, 22; exercises, 166–182; play, 185–205; skills, 40–42
simultaneous orgasm, spontaneous, 19–20

simultaneous orgasms in popular literature, 33–37
simultaneous orgasms, devaluing, 26–32
Solo Ejaculation Awareness (exercise for men), 157
Solo Multiple Orgasm (exercise for men), 159–160
sperm, 2, 3
spirituality, 5
Start and Stop: Peaking with a Partner (exercise for men), 90–91
Stream of Consciousness: The Ultimate Trust and Intimacy Builder (exercise), 204–206;
stretching, 65–66
sweating, 62
Switching Focus with Your Partner During Mutual Oral Sex (exercise), 197–198;
Switching Focus with Your Partner (exercise), 196–197
Switching Focus with Yourself (exercise), 196
Szaz, Thomas, 28

T

Tensing/Relaxing (exercise), 69
testosterone, 8, 61, 64
Thurber, James, 13
Tom Jones Dinner (exercise), 191–192
Towel Over His Face (exercise for women), 137–138
Trident Position (exercise), 107–108
triggers, 81, 173–175
trust, 192–195
Tuning in to Your Arousal (exercise for men), 85
Tuttle, Lisa, 140

U

unisex culture, 31–32
Using the PC Muscle for Control (exercise), 105–106

V

vagina, 124, 125
Vaginal Orgasms (exercise for women), 127–129
vaginisimus, 31
vibrators, 125, 126
visualizations, 44–45, 49–50
vitality, 62–63
vulnerability, 16

W

What Women and Men Really Want, 15
women and orgasm, 115–144
world peace, 11

Y

Your Inner Guide (exercise), 193

Hunter House
SEXUALITY

SEXUAL PLEASURE: Reaching New Heights of Sexual Arousal and Intimacy *by* Barbara Keesling, Ph.D.

> " For anyone who wishes to increase the ability to experience sensual pleasure." —***Yoga Journal***

First, here's what *Sexual Pleasure* is not: a general, use your fantasies, get romantic, light-some-incense, create-a-mind-set-for-good-love-and-it-will-happen kind of book. *Sexual Pleasure* is one of a kind. It starts with the first principle of intimacy: to experience deep sexual pleasure, you must explore your ability to enjoy — openly and sexually enjoy — basic human touch and relaxed, anxiety-free caressing.

This book shows you how to fully appreciate the pleasure of touching and being touched. It takes you through a series of stimulating exercises done both with and without a partner to increase your sensual awareness and experience sexual ecstasy. *Sexual Pleasure* is unique because it encourages you to focus on your own sexual desire, rather than looking for ways to please your partner. Being more in touch with what you enjoy leads naturally to greater passion, greater sensitivity, and greater pleasure for you both.

Sexual Pleasure is for everyone interested in experiencing lovemaking as a supremely pleasurable emotional and physical exchange, and in exploring the power of a deeply satisfying sex life. The exercises in this book can be used by people of any sexual orientation, and by those who may have physical limitations, or who are just learning about their sexuality — anyone seeking the secrets of strong and fulfilling sex.

Special topics include:

- **For women** — new methods on how to have orgasms more easily using your internal and external trigger points
- **For men** — how to prolong erections and synchronize orgasm and ejaculation for intense pleasure
- How women can have instant orgasms with their partner, or stimulate the G spot to have a "gusher"
- New masturbation techniques for men that will increase their penis sensitivity
- Favorite ways to play with your partner, increase intimacy, and achieve mutual arousal

For information on author Dr. Barbara Keesling, please see the following page.

224 pages ... 14 b/w photos ... Paperback $13.95 ... Hard cover $21.95

To order please see last page or call (800) 266-5592

Hunter House
SEXUALITY

MAKING LOVE BETTER THAN EVER: Exploring New Ways to Sexual Pleasure *by* Barbara Keesling, Ph.D.

Continually striving for new experiences and intimacy within a relationship is crucial to keeping the relationship growing and thriving. *Making Love Better than Ever* is for loving couples looking for sexual adventure within their monogamous relationship. In it author Dr. Barbara Keesling offers practical knowledge and rare insight about lovemaking in a warm, encouraging tone. Drawing from years of professional experience, Dr. Barbara Keesling explores the profound, complex, and soulful powers of sexuality. She explains that sexual exchange between loving partners provides all the elements for a happy, healthy life: touch, intimacy, communication, physical activity, and playfulness.

With the goal of improving this exchange and deepening the bond between lovers, Keesling provides a series of relaxation, body-image, and touch exercises that progress from simple to advanced. Some are designed to be done with a partner, some by oneself, and all can be performed by adults of any age, sexual orientation, and level of fitness.

Separate chapters discuss: how to have fun during sex; how sex can boost the immune system and even affect the look of one's hair, skin, and eyes; how to improve and maintain the physical toning necessary for a good sex life. Keesling's approach is backed by her work as a surrogate and therapist, as well as by anecdotes of real people's problems, experiences, and reactions, and topics clearly presented and explained. As she says, her book is "for people who want something more than just a sex manual. It is for those . . . who want to learn to make love in the deepest sense of the word — not just with their bodies, but with their hearts, minds, and souls."

Barbara Keesling, Ph.D., earned her doctorate in Health Psychology from the University of California and taught college courses for many years, lecturing on a variety of psychological topics. Her books include *Sexual Pleasure, Making Love Better than Ever, How to Make Love All Night* and *Talk Sexy to the One You Love.* She has contributed to or been featured in journals including *Redbook, Cosmopolitan,* and *Men's Health.* She has appeared on hundreds of television and radio shows including "Geraldo," "The Howard Stern Show," and "Real Personal." Dr. Keesling has been called everything from "The Martha Stewart of Sex" to "the first therapist who looks like she's actually had sex!"

256 pages ... 15 illus. ... Paperback ... $13.95 ... Available January 1998

For a FREE catalog of books call (800) 266-5592

Hunter House
PERSONAL GROWTH, SEXUALITY

THE PLEASURE PRESCRIPTION: To Love, to Work, to Play — Life in the Balance by Paul Pearsall, Ph.D.
New York Times **Bestseller!**

This bestselling book is a prescription for stressed out lives. Dr. Pearsall maintains that contentment, wellness, and long life can be found by devoting time to family, helping others, and slowing down to savor life's pleasures. Pearsall's unique approach draws from Polynesian wisdom and his own 25 years of psychological and medical research. For readers who want to discover a way of life that promotes healthy values and living, *The Pleasure Prescription* provides the answers.

288 pages ... Paperback $13.95 ... Hard cover $23.95

WOMEN, SEX & DESIRE: Exploring Your Sexuality at Every Stage of Life by Elizabeth Davis, Foreword by Germaine Greer

Women, Sex & Desire explores all aspects of women's sexuality and sexual health. Author Elizabeth Davis describes the cycles of a woman's sexuality, combining intriguing facts and little-known biological information with descriptions of rituals from other cultures, time-honored herbal treatments, and personal stories.

224 pages ... 9 illus. ... Paperback $12.95 ... Hard cover $22.95

THE A-TO-Z OF WOMEN'S SEXUALITY
by Ada P. Kahn and Linda Hughey Holt, M.D.

This sensitively written book sorts out the information on women's sexuality in a clear, jargon-free style. With over 2000 alphabetically arranged entries, this resource has cross-referenced entries on subjects such as female and male sexual response cycles, gynecological tests, medications, and contraception methods.

368 pages ... 19 illus. ... Paperback ... $14.95

THE FERTILITY AWARENESS HANDBOOK: The Natural Guide to Avoiding or Achieving Pregnancy
by Barbara Kass-Annese, R.N., and Hal Danzer, M.D.

By charting the natural language of the body, women can track the days of the month when they are most fertile and most likely to conceive, or when they are infertile and can safely have intercourse without conceiving. These noninvasive techniques have no frightening side effects and teach women how to be more in touch with their bodies and well-being.

176 pages ... 47 illus. ... Paperback ... $11.95

Prices subject to change

ORDER FORM

10% DISCOUNT on orders of $50 or more –
20% DISCOUNT on orders of $150 or more –
30% DISCOUNT on orders of $500 or more –
On cost of books for fully prepaid orders

NAME

ADDRESS

CITY/STATE   ZIP/POSTCODE

PHONE   COUNTRY

TITLE	QTY	PRICE	TOTAL
Simultaneous Orgasm (paperback)		@ $14.95	
Sexual Pleasure (paperback)		@ $13.95	
Making Love Better than Ever (paperback)		@ $13.95	
Please list other titles below:			
		@ $	
		@ $	
		@ $	
		@ $	
		@ $	
		@ $	
		@ $	

Shipping costs
First book: $3.00 by book post; $4.50 by UPS or to ship outside the U.S.
Each additional book: $1.00
For rush orders and bulk shipments call us at (800) 266-5592

SUBTOTAL
Less discount @ _____ %   (_____)
TOTAL COST OF BOOKS
Calif. residents add sales tax
Shipping & handling
TOTAL ENCLOSED
Please pay in U.S. funds only

❏ Check   ❏ Money Order   ❏ Visa   ❏ M/C   ❏ Discover

Card # _____   Exp date _____

Signature _____

Complete and mail to:
Hunter House Inc., Publishers
PO Box 2914, Alameda CA 94501-0914
Orders: 1-800-266-5592 . . . ordering@hunterhouse.com
Phone (510) 865-5282 Fax (510) 865-4295
❏ Check here to receive our FREE book catalog